We Built an
Oak Frame House
in Cornwall

by

Chris and Jan Stevens

Grosvenor House
Publishing Limited

This book is published by
Grosvenor House Publishing Ltd
Link House
140 The Broadway, Tolworth, Surrey, KT6 7HT.
www.grosvenorhousepublishing.co.uk

A CIP record for this book
is available from the British Library

ISBN 978-1-83975-621-4

For Simon and Hannah
With much Love

'Nothing great in the world has been
accomplished without passion.'
(Hegel 1832)

(Complemented by talent, hard work and tenacity!)

CONTENTS

FOREWORD

ESSENTIAL reading .... particularly if you're contemplating building your own house.

As a Chartered Surveyor, I have been involved with property in one way or another for the last 55 years, including advising Chris and Jan on various house sales and projects. Coincidentally, we self-built our house some 40 years ago, obviously much younger, probably less able, with two pre-school boys, whilst running my own professional company. Weekends and evenings until midnight were the norm and we reckon it took two years to get over it! However, we are still here, having made a few additions with minimal alterations to the original plans. How this book would have been essential bedtime reading!

Having the desire to build your own home is obviously a given; but you must also have vision, guts, tenacity, drive and be prepared for relentless hard work. Essential prior planning, forensic attention to detail and patient man-management skills .... you are on a conveyor belt that you can't get off; and a bit of luck along the way is always welcome.

It goes without saying that Chris and Jan have these attributes in spades. Chris taught both our sons, and Sue my wife, taught with him often and recalls that same intelligence, attention to detail and discipline that he has brought to all their building endeavours.

This book is an incisive step-by-step guide through such projects, outlining the pitfalls, including underwhelming professional help, Planning issues and the resulting financial implications .... and then you throw COVID into the mix.

However, none of this derailed their ambitions and evidenced by the photos, they have achieved a truly amazing house, built to extremely high standards, in an enviable and unique spot.

Their book is a well-written, immensely practical guide to building your own house, that also happens to be a fascinating read, and should be by your side as you embark on one of the most exhilarating and scary challenges of your life. Simply indispensable.

Well done, Chris and Jan. Now .... relax!

David Balment, April 2021
Fellow of the Royal Institution of Chartered Surveyors

PREFACE

In 1996 we embarked upon what became a twenty-five year building programme, developing more than 1,000 square metres of buildings in Cornwall. This was to be a second career; we are Teachers and at the start we had limited DIY skills. The first two projects involved iconic 19th century agricultural barn conversions and the final project, essentially completed in 2020, was a sustainable, green oak new-build. Remarkably, all three major builds were initially rejected by either Planners or a Structural Engineer. This book describes the challenges and rewards of a self-build oak frame house. Can you benefit from our experience?

Opting to self-build is certainly one of the big decisions in life. Some like ourselves, have fulfilled this a number of times as our circumstances have changed. Inevitably, you will encounter many difficulties and stresses before any rewards materialise. What can you expect during this self-build process? This book offers an honest appraisal of self-build, not in the hope of persuading you to start this journey, but to open your eyes to the very real challenges that you will encounter.

Are you one of the '7 million Brits ..... currently researching the process of building their own homes'?[*] This large number is supported by the Building Societies Association, stating that nearly a third (32%) of GB adults are interested in designing and building their own home. These are dreams and for many will remain so; but if more people can be encouraged through

---

[*] build-review.com, April 2019

Government incentives, assisted mortgages and motivational books(!), then there will be two significant achievements. Firstly, self-builders will contribute enormously to reducing the current housing crisis. Secondly, thousands of people will create homes that will probably be of a higher specification and value than they would have otherwise achieved; a home that they will be immensely proud of.

ACKNOWLEDGEMENTS

Roger and Alan: We are indebted to your skilled contribution to this build. Roger, you provided an accurate and sound foundation and a structure that we could build onto. Alan, you are an extremely accomplished finisher and nothing seemed to faze you. We thank you both in equal measure.

Andrew Holloway and Green Oak Carpentry team: Your patience, encouragement and expertise set you apart. Jamie and yard/field team, your ears should be burning; sun protection lotion was the least that we could provide for such a great team!

Richard Ward, Pentargon Architecture: Thank you for transforming our sketches in collaboration with Green Oak Carpentry into a worthy set of professional plans for an aesthetically-admired, sustainable home.

Brian, Danny and Jerry, J J Smith & Co Joinery Ltd: You and the workshop produced quality joinery on time. You are always positive; thank you. Sean and Kayan: Probably the best slating pair in Cornwall! Mark, Phil and Jake: A quality finish from a reliable, flexible, efficient, plastering team. Nathan Martin, Adept Glass: You came, you measured and you delivered great service, thank you. Jonathan Coyle, Harvest Cornwall: You secured the project with your initial knowledgeable guidance, backed with Aaron's practical expertise. David Warr, Plumber: Endless enthusiasm and care. Ryan Skews, 'Sparky': Thank you, Ryan for picking up the electrics from a distance; a project of which you can be proud. Bruce and the workshop, Camel Joinery Ltd: Thank you for a well-crafted set of stairs and balustrade.

Geraldine, Mike and Sue, Trevor and Shirley, Ray and Family: We have appreciated your support over the years with practical assistance and positivity.

Simon, Hannah, Serena and Alistair: Your support, professionally, practically and emotionally is cherished.

Finally, David Balment, FRICS: An obvious choice to provide a Foreword for this book. You have been a longstanding friend for nearly forty years, during which time you have provided sound professional advice on various matters concerning buildings. Your lifetime experience of surveying and house marketing has been heeded; thank you David.

INTRODUCTION

We are not developers or even builders, let alone tradespeople; but that has not prevented us from converting and building in excess of 1,000 square metres over a 25-year period. There have been three major builds and what is remarkable is that all three were initially rejected by either Planners or a Structural Engineer. This has resulted in challenges which inevitably have morphed into experience, lots of it! Our hope and aim is to inspire and motivate anyone who wishes to achieve the wonderful dream of building your own home. You can do this and we hope that this book will make the journey a little easier than it might have been. When you have achieved your constructed home, you know that you deserve the title 'Self-build Warrior'!

It is evident from the chapter headings that there is plenty of detailed information, ideas and advice. Building your own house will also require a quality that only you can determine that you possess, that is a degree of tenacity. You can't buy it and we don't think you can go on a course to acquire it. Optimistically, most of us have some and we believe that it is reinforced with experience. After all, according to that well-known adage, 'What doesn't kill you, makes you stronger', tenacity will help in the hundreds of decisions necessary in a build. Negotiations involving a few pence on the price of a metre of batten and other materials, will soon translate into hundreds of pounds of savings throughout the build.

On a far more serious note, at the start of our build experience in 1996, converting a large barn complex, we were faced with the threat of being sued when the relationship with our initial Architect turned sour. This action was particularly galling because we had always been determined to engage architectural expertise for advice and protection, as a safeguard against bad practice and financial ruin. The threat of a court case naturally caused considerable anxiety, that is until we sought advice from a Solicitor who recommended that we counter-sue, based on our narrative and the strength of our convictions. We were given the courage to diligently prepare our own case with the confidence to present it in Court, if required. The Architect withdrew his case following a preliminary Court hearing in the presence of the Judge. Please don't be scared by this; being sued is rare. It has rather, taught us that such bullying behaviour from a professional or company can be dealt with, if you are prepared to put in the time to check, research and carefully present your evidence. The whole experience has had a positive effect on us in the way that we deal with eventualities and have managed further build projects.

Our first project: iconic agricultural barns in East Cornwall

Our first project, a 500 square metre, 19th century barn complex in the countryside, was to be a home, together with quite a large Children's Nursery. This had land to accommodate outside play activities, complete with a stream, vineyard, raised beds for flowers and vegetables, together with a range of animals. It was a wonderful, if ambitious first project which almost fell at the outset when a Local Planning Officer gave the proposal of a Children's Nursery on part of the site, an initial thumbs down with a telephone response of, "I shouldn't think so!" We had a stark choice, accept the advice and continue the considerable search for another suitable property or show some tenacity by tackling the issue head-on. The solution became evident following a discussion with a female Planning Officer in the days when informal visits to the Local Planning Office were permitted. She was more sympathetic to the proposal, living up to the positive 'can do' slogan emblazoned on the Reception walls! The advice from the Planning Officer was to ensure that we fulfilled particular policy guidelines by proving a need for childcare within the locality. Conducting a community questionnaire was our solution, to establish Early Years Education requirements in the area. The response was positive and the existing residential Planning Permission was changed to a combination of residential and business use, exclusively for the Nursery.

The second project, a Grade II Listed, 19th century barn, had an equally dubious start. This derelict barn similarly came with residential Planning Permission and therefore included a set of plans that had been passed by Planning. However, on subsequent investigation, a height issue became evident in maintaining two floors. Our Structural Engineer, on visiting the site stated emphatically that the proposed conversion couldn't be achieved! A good friend, the accomplished builder that had been significantly involved in the residential part of our former project, had a much more positive approach. The Conservation Officer did not permit the height of the roof to be increased; our solution was to go down. Approximately 100 tonnes of shillet (relatively loose rock) were removed to create a two-storey barn conversion of aesthetically-pleasing proportions. We built outside the box! Once again, it demonstrated that solutions can be found with a tenacious and inventive approach. We continually find that a positive attitude goes a long way in life.

Our second project: Grade II Listed barn in North Cornwall

Our final project, the oak frame new-build, has been a long-held dream. The plot of land that we were attempting to buy, further west in Cornwall, required the sale of the linhay barn, which did not go well. The new-build was threatening to slip through our fingers. An Estate Agent friend (see Foreword) offered us some professional guidance, indicating that it all boiled down to where we wanted to be in a few years' time. His lifetime experience was heeded and we managed to finally pull-off a decisive sale, enabling us to commit our energy to a building plot that once again had full, permanent, residential Planning Permission. Once again, there was a major snag. The initial Planning Permission was for a 14-metre diameter eco-dome! This dome, originally classified for holiday use, had been described as a 'unique tourist experience'. We felt confident in dealing with the necessary design changes to suit a permanent residence, considering our past experience with Planning. However, our Planning Permission Application for an oak frame residence was categorically refused, without negotiation. The Local Authority comments had indicated that only a dome would do on this site. This was unbelievable! We knew that this was contrary to the

National Planning Policy. In true determined spirit, an Appeal was lodged with the independent Government body. The Local Authority decision was overturned, not without criticism.

These particular battles took place over a period of about twenty years. We have recorded them, not to scare or dissuade you from pursuing your dream, but rather to prepare you for what may have to be faced.

Let's switch the focus, momentarily. What is your current motivation for building your own home? Perhaps you have been enticed by the many television series which, more often than not, conclude that considerable financial returns can be achieved. The seasoned wisdom of the building industry refers to the 'rule of three'; the aim is to spend one third on the plot, one third on the build, leaving the final third as profit when the house is sold. We caution that some of the valuations in these programmes are woefully optimistic and are not representative of the actual selling prices achieved if the property were to be sold. In our experience, quality plots have significantly risen in value, as have building materials and labour costs. Besides, if you are looking to sell on, do you qualify as a self-builder or a developer? In our experience, most self-builders are motivated by saving rather than making money. The saving equation is determined by the amount of time that you invest into the build. Honesty is important here. Assuming that you earn £30,000 a year and you devote two years of your time to your build, as opposed to employment, that earning deficit should be costed-in. We believe that in most instances, it is not.

To self-build can mean everything from achieving the majority of the building yourself, to using a main contractor and perhaps merely selecting final finish items such as taps and paint colour. In reality, very few people have all the skills to achieve all of the work themselves; besides such a project would take many years to fulfil! It is a balance of doing the work that you are able to do and paying others to assist. Some self-builders even hold down a day job while committing to work on the build in the evenings and at the weekends. The advantage here of course is that the income can help to fund the build; but it can be detrimental to family, health and relationships.

In the great variety of TV shows on building houses, the term Project Manager is often used. Basically, someone has to organise the construction, plan the sequence of tasks, order materials and liaise with Building Control etc. Self-builders habitually take on this role, although if you are employing a Main Contractor or Builder (see Chapter 5 on Build Routes) they will normally assume Project Management responsibility. This is one of the reasons why you pay more for their services. There is absolutely no reason why a first-time self-builder should not Project Manage, providing time is allowed and there is an awareness of hints and suggestions from the more experienced members of the team.

'New skills can be developed, depending upon the degree of involvement ……. to achieve something special.'

A common thread running through articles and programmes is the acknowledgement that the self-builder can achieve a house that they probably could not afford to buy. Additionally, a self-builder can have a significant design input. New skills can be developed, depending upon the degree of involvement. It will be a project that you will eat and breathe for probably more than a year and perhaps two or more. The motivation to self-build is a great deal more than financial; it is to be creative to achieve something special.

Our advice is to try to surround yourself with positive people, capable of problem-solving and constructive ideas. Be tenacious in your dealings with individuals, commercial enterprises and Local Authorities. Above all, stay strong and pursue your dream. Self-build warriors, go for it!

CHAPTER 1

Why an Oak Frame?

From the outset, let us be clear, we built an oak-framed house, we did not build the oak frame. This was achieved by a company with many years of experience with green oak. It was an involved process of design, in collaboration with ourselves, Green Oak Carpentry and our new, local (friendly!) Architect. The frame was constructed by a team in a large building at the woodyard in Hampshire, then taken apart and transported to our site in Cornwall.

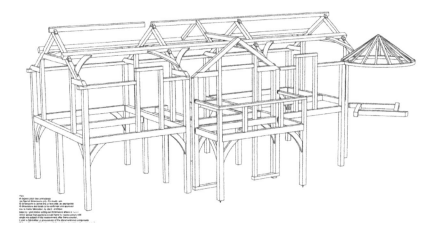

The design of the oak frame:
The Green Oak Carpentry Company Ltd

In a nutshell, one of the essential reasons for choosing an oak frame is that it is eco-friendly. Growing trees absorb carbon dioxide and providing every tree that is removed for construction is replaced by five others, this absorption rate is sustained; a similar justification applies to Christmas trees. In contrast, standard UK house construction involves the use of thousands of concrete blocks or bricks and requires more energy for production and transportation.

A second response to the question concerning an oak frame construction, is that it is aesthetically-pleasing. It is a traditional building type where you can clearly identify the construction method, including the securing wooden pegs. There is also an advantage in gaining a head start in achieving your defined spaces, as the frame will be erected in a matter of days. The process of adding the softwood skin of stud, plywood and insulation can commence straight away. This is a methodical, rather than a particularly skilled process which lends itself to the self-builder. Structurally Insulated Panels, known as SIPs are often chosen for this process which is speedy, but add greatly to the self-build costs. Oak frame construction therefore, has many advantages.

Construction of tower roof in Green Oak Carpentry workshop in Hampshire

We were drawn to the fact that this would be a 'new building' as opposed to our previous two projects which were conversions of old stone barns. Although craftsmen of previous centuries used a square and a level in construction, the years have taken their toll on these old structures, giving rise to quirkiness, which is euphemistically described as 'having character'. You have to adapt and compromise as you renovate and modernise. This was often a challenge, especially when a certain Conservation Officer tried to insist on retaining a sloping 14-metre long floor; marbles, billiard tables and chairs on castors would all be no-noes! Since the floorboards and floor joists needed replacing, we eventually got our way. Building new was a novel experience compared to past quirky conversion projects, although with green oak, allowances are still needed for shrinkage, shakes and twists which occur relatively quickly once the oak frame is protected from the elements.

Our more specific personal preference for this style was based on a formative experience in our early Teaching careers, living in a quintessential small town in West Sussex. Half-timbered buildings, many dating back to the fifteenth century are an essential feature of the townscape, typically celebrated in paintings, on postcards and sweet boxes. The buildings of this region have such a historical significance that a number that were in danger of neglect, collapse or redevelopment have been painstakingly dismantled and re-erected in imaginative settings at the Singleton Open Air Museum. Innumerable appearances of this museum in documentaries, films and educational programmes, demonstrate the authenticity of this conservation and restoration work. We cannot overestimate how such powerful images have resurfaced to exert their influence on us, decades on. Furthermore, the research and innovative use of traditional materials, culminating in the construction of the futuristic Downland Gridshell at Singleton, has brought such influence to an international audience. Unaware to us at the time, our Green Oak Company had constructed this state-of-the-art structure. We had discussed our project with many oak frame companies across the country. The Green Oak Company was chosen because of their genuine enthusiasm, along with their obvious expertise and a favourable financial quotation. The oak frame accounted for approaching 25% of our total build cost; a significant consideration.

CHAPTER 2

The Plot

> 'Buy land, they're not making it anymore.'
>
> Mark Twain

We discovered our plot advertised online. On viewing the site, it had been subdivided into two prospective plots, one with and one without Planning Permission. We purchased it as one complete plot. The existing residential Planning Permission for a 14-metre diameter dome related to a much larger project. The second proposed plot, without Planning Permission, contained an 18th century ruin of a former Estate Manager's dwelling. The owner seemed to think that we wanted to renovate the ruin, rather than build a new house!

**The oak frame plot:
a sloping site but with impressive views**

It was a south-facing, sloping site totalling a fraction over an acre, irregular in shape. Having viewed and rejected hundreds of plots over a number of years of searching, this one had the least number of compromises. Access was good, electricity was on site with a water supply on the boundary. There was no contaminated land, it was not in a flood hazard zone, there were picturesque river views and an abundance of trees. The site ticked so many of the boxes compared with others. Furthermore, the situation of the plot was ideal, with all the facilities of an urban centre, all within walking distance; that is twenty-five minutes into town at a leisurely pace and thirty-five minutes back uphill. Whilst within the urban boundary, the overwhelming feeling was one of being in the countryside. In fact, anyone using satnav to locate us often arrives via a very circuitous, rural route .... and they wonder where the centre is!

We regarded the ruin as an asset to the plot, whereas the sloping nature of the site was a definite negative for building, particularly as we had a pre-existing idea of the house that we wanted to build. Most self-builders, given the choice, would opt for a level site to avoid difficulties of construction and the ensuing extra cost. Building sites are often exercises in compromise of location, price and access of services. Even a gentle slope will require significant construction decisions in so many unforeseen ways, bearing in mind that floors need to be level but drainage, either foul or rainwater, will require gradients.

There are three basic techniques used to deal with sloping sites. Firstly, retain the slope and design the house around it. The advantages would be the views and perhaps an integrated undercroft garage, although the suspended floors and the sophisticated foundations would be more expensive. Alternatively, and in contrast to placing the house on the slope, a level site can

Three Ways of Building on a Sloping Site

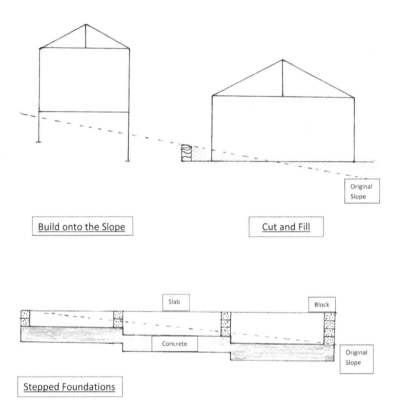

Build onto the Slope

Cut and Fill

Original Slope

Slab

Block

Concrete

Original Slope

Stepped Foundations

be created by the process of 'cut and fill', moving excavated upslope material to the lower slope. The cut will often require a retaining wall, along with some stabilisation on the lower slope. This process produces a significant volume of material and unless the plot has substantial space around it, this will have to be removed, potentially at considerable expense. The final method of overcoming the sloping issue is digging stepped foundations, which involves staggering the foundation trenches downhill. Blockwork is then used to bring the foundations level, with some of the excavated material from the trenches used as infill.

Stepped foundation trenches:
note deep hole for tower foundation

'Cut and fill' in action

Our photographs show that we used a combination of cut and fill and stepped foundations to achieve a level site. This required the expertise of a proficient groundworker, given that our plot sloped to the south and east. Great care was needed in damming the staggered trenches and pouring the concrete to the correct levels. The entire process from breaking ground to the pouring of 'the slab' essentially took two full-time people plus some extra help, eight weeks to complete; but not everyone would have the complications of a tower on a sloping site!

Stone ruin on plot: a great source of stone and brick buried in collapsed walls

The stone ruin enhances the setting of our building and we have used a great deal of natural stone in the house construction, which blends the two. It is thought that this ruin fell into disrepair in the interwar years and much of the stone was 'robbed'. Subsequent decay and collapse has left a treasure trove of buried stone and brick, freely available for retrieval with a pick and shovel. The time interval between purchasing the plot and 'breaking ground', well over two years, due to Planning and other issues, was partly used to excavate the material. Much of the tower is built of this

15

stone with some handmade bricks, originally made on the farm, hundreds of years ago.

Following the viewing of the plot, we sat by the river. It was peaceful and beautiful. We discussed the pros and cons. It was a short discussion. After around ten years of searching, we were convinced from the outset that we had discovered our 'forever' plot. All sites come with compromises and the skill is to make the most of the attributes offered. Once secured you can unleash your aspirations, subject to Planning, of course!

CHAPTER 3

Design Considerations

Our children had flown the nest and therefore we concentrated on what we wanted and needed from such a build. The essential wish list was a two-storey, three-bed, rectangular box with four additional features to enhance the design. The first was a double-height atrium space, with a walkway at first floor level to access the bedrooms and bathrooms, enabling a further appreciation of the vaulted ceilings. It also provided a fabulous vantage point for the beautiful views of the river across a sloping woodland. Another feature that we were determined to include, was a stone tower to provide an entrance lobby on the ground floor, together with a reading room off the master bedroom; once again providing spectacular views of the river and trees from different aspects. At the rear of the building, we added the utility and plant room and ground floor WC. The addition of the fourth element, a balcony, was the only design feature that we had some concerns with. The leisure benefits of such a structure were obvious, but would it reduce the light in the lounge? We return to the balcony issue in Chapter 15 on energy. Essentially then, we built a three-bed, two-storey house with some special additions.

Externally, we wanted our house to blend into the rural, wooded landscape. 'Eco' demanded natural materials, with slate used for the roof and a proportion of the walls and larch cladding with a stone plinth up to the slate window sills. Yes, there is a large area of glass on the south elevation, but that relates to the reduction of the carbon footprint; an eco-friendly approach does have its compromises. We are greatly encouraged by the frequent positive comments about the external appearance of our building, invariably echoing our aim from the outset to harmonize the house with its surroundings. However, in the Planning process (Chapter 4) our

June 2019: Our new house nearing completion, illustrating two
of the special design features, the tower and the balcony.
Note the unweathered Siberian larch cladding.

April 2021: Note mellow colour of Siberian larch cladding,
together with other natural materials of stone, slate and brick.

building was labelled 'incongruous'. Such divergence of opinion would result in friction and inevitably lead to an arbitration process.

Too many self-builders fall into the trap of designing and constructing buildings that are significantly larger than they currently need and are surprised when the budget struggles to keep up with the invoices. This oak frame design was the smallest of our three projects; yes, we were downsizing. The lounge of our second barn project had internal dimensions of fourteen metres by six metres and we adopted this size as the basic footprint, enabling us to plot and walk through the layout. We also constructed a scale model to appreciate the proportions of our proposed design. When we were satisfied with the results, basic sketches of internal layouts and external elevations (the outside appearance) of the building were drawn. These were then handed over to a local Architect to produce plans to be submitted for Planning Permission and to present to the Green Oak Frame Company for initial discussion.

Our Architect in Cornwall was not experienced in designing oak frame buildings and consequently, at the suggestion of our Hampshire-based Oak Frame Company, we arranged for him to attend a collaborative meeting with us at the woodyard. This meeting achieved the marrying of our requirements and aspirations for the build with the practicalities of the oak frame structure. Many companies that produce oak frames have in-house designers and architects to draw plans for Planning Permission as part of a complete package.

A small digression is necessary here to reinforce the idea of maintaining positive people and companies in the fulfilment of your dream. The Green Oak Company has remained enthusiastic about our oak frame aspirations over many years. The following illustrative anecdote also indicates how important it is to keep a tape measure handy! During our intensive search for that elusive building plot, we discovered an enticing site in Wadebridge, one of our favourite Cornish centres on the River Camel and close to some fabulous beaches. The plot had outline residential Planning Permission and we kick-started a similar process of initial discussion with our Green Oak Company, before pegging out the footprint of our proposed building on the generous plot, described as approaching half an acre. It soon became evident that the house couldn't be comfortably positioned on the site; either the house was too big or the plot was too small! The estate agent reiterated that the plot was just under half an acre in size. Unconvinced, we commissioned a digital survey which confirmed the size as just under a third of an acre, effectively a quarter of an acre plus a drive. The estate agent was disinterested in the discrepancy and we withdrew our interest. It was not the first time that building plots had been misrepresented. The Green Oak Company, when informed of our disappointing news, accepted that these things happen and looked forward to future contact when we succeeded in finding that special plot. They have been encouraging throughout over a significant number of years!

Eastern elevation illustrating natural materials:
recycled stone, slate and brick

The Tower

We have built an oak frame house; but the first impression on approaching from the old eastern entrance is ironically, of the stone-built tower. Recycled stone, slate and bricks, greying oak lintels, together with a backdrop of an 18th century ruin, deceive the eye as to its very recent construction.

"Is it Listed?"
"Did you have a bat issue?"
"Did you construct the oak frame onto an older building?"

These are all comments by socially-distanced passers-by who were generally exploring new, local jaunts during the 2020 Covid epidemic Lockdown. We graciously accepted the questions as compliments, particularly as we set out from the start to produce a building that blended into its rural, wooded surroundings and indeed the neighbourhood; a point that was definitely lost on our Local Authority Planning team!

**Serlio floor structure in tower:
note weatherproofing polythene on exterior**

Self-builders often enthusiastically indulge in creative elements; but so did the Green Oak Company. In addition to the entire oak frame structure of the house, they inspirationally incorporated serlio* ceiling/floor timbers into the design of the tower, together with a magnificent three-metre diameter oak ring-beam and rafter ceiling. This is a real triumph of their craft.

The addition of a stone tower to an oak frame is quite unusual. We were clearly influenced by a new house with a tower that we became interested in purchasing following the sale of our first barn complex, together with an enduring fascination for windmill towers on Mediterranean islands and follies** in Southern England. Our tower is not a folly in that it has created two very useful, characterful spaces; although, as realised from the outset it has taken a disproportionate amount of time and money, not to mention head-scratching on how to achieve it, as illustrated in the photo sequence Chapter 10. We are so pleased that we included this extravagance.

---

* serlio: '....... spanning a space with beams, none of which is long enough to reach clear across ....' (Cambridge University Press)
** folly: 'a costly ornamental building with no practical purpose' (Oxford Languages)

CHAPTER 4

Planning

There are three 'Ps' that are crucial to any new self-build, that is Plot and Planning Permission; without these your aspiration will remain a dream. Building plots are difficult to find; good plots are rare and often don't appear in the public domain. We spent ten years searching and our second barn conversion was in fact the result of this frustrated search.

We found the current plot, as previously mentioned, late one evening on the internet, viewed it at the earliest opportunity and realised that this was the one. A variety of complications were ironed out and the deal was eventually secured. We were on our way to building our dream, our oak frame building; or so we thought! We purchased the plot in November 2014 and did not 'break ground' until February 2017 due to a combination of factors: the realisation of our financial assets and Planning issues. Tenacity was required in spades!

Our building plot had permanent residential Planning Permission. However, this was for a 14-metre diameter eco-dome, one of seven holiday domes originally described by the Local Authority as a 'unique tourist experience' which formed part of a larger project. Our plot, which was physically separated from the other six, was subsequently granted permanent residential Planning Permission, replacing holiday use. The resulting upgrade in value was to provide the 'enabling' finance for the development of the rest of the scheme. We had some planning experience and understood that once a plot had achieved permanent residential Planning Permission, the design of the proposed building could be negotiated with Planning Authorities. This is clearly set out in National Planning Policy documents. We confidently submitted our Planning Application for a more conventional house, anticipating that some compromise may be needed.

To our shock, utter disbelief and contrary to Planning rules, the Local Authority refused to negotiate, insisting that only a dome would do on this site. At one point, we were even informed that the existing Planning Permission had expired, which was an erroneous statement. We were given a few weeks to withdraw our Planning Application to avoid a refusal. Subsequently, we realised that this was advantageous to the Local Authority because they would avoid the recording of a refusal statistic. We did not withdraw the Application, Planning Permission was refused and the only choice remaining was either to build the 14-metre diameter dome or to submit a Planning Appeal to the independent Government Authority.

Despite having submitted a variety of Planning Permissions over a twenty-year period, none had ever been refused; so we had never faced the challenge of lodging an Appeal. We realised that we were reaching the limit of our Planning knowledge and expertise, but were able to call upon professional advice from a family member who had additional Planning contacts. The consensus was that we were facing incomprehensible intransigence! Our draft Appeal was adjusted to follow the advised format; a factual account that avoided emotive issues. We gratefully acknowledge the positivity of this specialist help and support, given the perceived failure of the Planning procedures. Our Appeal was successful; but particularly galling was the statement by the Appeal Officer that the Local Authority had embellished* their data in refusing our Application. Our reaction was that at best we had been treated unfairly and the financial implications of the resulting delay were costly for us.

---

* embellished: overstated/exaggerated/to make a statement more applicable by adding extra details that are often untrue

CHAPTER 5

The Budget

This is your house that you are building; it is your dream. Often your ideas could be enhanced and developed by Architects and Designers. Just make sure that their aspirations don't become your financial nightmare!

Most of us will have played 'Monopoly' and enjoyed buying houses and hotels! In the real World, as in the game, acquisitions and development require cash, mortgages and income in various combinations. TV programmes often show projects that go seriously over budget, despite all the advice that is available. It should be a simple calculation of how much money you have and how much house you can build for this amount, allowing for a contingency fund. Fortunately, there are cost calculators and tables to assist with this calculation, based on costs per square metre. The 'Homebuilding and Renovating' magazine references a calculator* which takes into account the region, number of storeys, size of building, quality of craftsmanship, materials and selected finishes. It also takes into consideration how much of the work you intend to do yourself. There are four main build routes:

Build Route A: DIY and Sub-contractors
"   "   B: Sub-contractors
"   "   C: Main Builder and Sub-contractors
"   "   D: Main Contractor

---

* https://www.homebuilding.co.uk/advice/calculator

Basically, the more work other people do, the greater the cost per square metre. There are three levels of build quality:

Standard: Typical estate house, including softwood joinery, contract kitchen, basic sanitaryware and central heating with radiators.

Good: Often underfloor heating, quality contract kitchen, higher specification for bathrooms.

Excellent: Typically, bespoke kitchen with granite surfaces, hardwood joinery with quality fixtures and fittings.

Such calculations will give you a fairly accurate guide to the cost of building your house. A contingency of at least 10% should be factored in for unforeseen expenditures. A Quantity Surveyor would perhaps give you peace of mind, although we have always trusted our instincts, along with careful budgeting. We have found that the Homebuilding and Renovating magazine, websites and shows have been an excellent source of inspiration, design, knowledge and products, throughout our three major builds.

Having set the budget, build route and quality, allowing a minimum 10% contingency, why do projects still drift, sometimes seriously, over budget? We suspect that a considerable number of self-builders construct the house that they are determined to create, which is often too big and then try to make the available funds work their magic. A recent conversation from a TV-build summed this up precisely: "We follow our hearts and hope the bank balance keeps up!" Given the scale of the finance, this is not a responsible approach.

Over-optimism and a lack of contingency then are two causes of budget drift. There are unfortunately, many more and not all can be anticipated. We had allocated the funds for the appropriate size of house, to an excellent quality. The tower added significantly to the budget but would be financed by surplus income over the two to three years of the build. We were determined to invest this income into a design feature that would truly enhance our home.

The tower: a design feature to truly enhance our home, although the cost per square metre is disproportionately higher than the main structure of the building.

Perhaps the most obvious 'hit' on the budget is inflation. If your build is scheduled to take two years and inflation is running at 3%, then you are already thousands of pounds down. In our case, many of the building material prices increased by more than the inflation rate. The price of insulation increased by 11%, supposedly due to a global shortage. On one occasion, the price of external slate sills jumped by 33%. When challenged, we were informed that we had been re-categorised from a trade to a domestic tariff. The company sensibly reverted to the former price. They would have lost all future custom had a sense of fairness not prevailed! It is generally accepted that a self-builder is a trade account customer.

Ignorance can increase your bills. We were blissfully unaware of the specialist tape required to secure the polythene bubble constructed within modern houses, bringing a price tag in excess of £500 for our build!

Your head must certainly keep an eye on the budget as your heart shops. Upgrades impact on the budget at all levels. A superior downlight may only cost a few pounds more, but some houses may have one hundred or more. In our case, we decided on a 'green' upgrade from an oil-fired boiler system to an air source heat pump (ASHP) at an extra cost of around three thousand pounds.

Gas, electricity, water, sewage and phone lines are all essential services; but getting them to the plot can be mega-expensive. Many developers and self-builders will also tell you that just 'getting out of the ground' is partly guesswork. The tower and south-east corner of our building required a three-metre deep excavation due to the discovery of clay rather than shillet. A great deal more block and concrete were required that we had not budgeted for, just to get back to the surface. 'What goes down, must come up!'

The weather can have a major impact on your budget. It could slow the build down or worse, ruin what you have done. All self-builders will have weather stories to tell; few of these will be positive. Related to this is the self-builder on a TV programme, proudly presenting a spreadsheet of a one-year build, with every week accounted for. The reaction of the presenter can be imagined, scoffing at the unrealistic precision. The unpredictable weather is one possible impact, another is the necessary 'sequencing' of tasks which can often be affected by delays in one of the trades. If in Week 30 of the schedule, the windows do not arrive on site, as frequently happens, you are not 'dry' for Week 31, fixing the plasterboard. This knock-on effect will have financial implications. One of the most frustrating parts of self-build is being let-down; something out of your control that affects the timetabling and livelihood of other tradespeople.

An infinite number of personal situations could impact on the budget. Funds may dry up or the unpredictability of an accident or illness may totally wipe out the contingency. The conclusion of our build in the first half of 2020, was severely impacted by the Covid 19 epidemic. We viewed our completed stairs in a local factory in mid-March. However, the subsequent National Lockdown prevented delivery until June. Our official 'completion' was delayed, which required an expensive, short-term extension of our Construction Insurance.

Finally, according to our experience, we would suggest a contingency figure of at least 1% for mistakes: misreading plans, remedial correction of materials and techniques, damage to equipment, usually requiring you to foot the bill, however unfair that may seem.

In summary, build what you can afford, allowing at least a 10% contingency for all the 'unknown unknowns'! Keep a very close eye on the money, bearing in mind that an overspend in one area will require compromise in another. There are enough concerns during the course of a build without money being one of them. It is always sad to hear of self-builders who do not want to visit the site because of money worries. Take and maintain control to make it an enjoyable build.

CHAPTER 6

Caravan Living

To caravan or not to caravan; that is the question!

Home for nearly two years!

We have lived on site in a static caravan for a total of two and a half years during two of our three build projects. On our first build we overwintered with our two young children. The current build has included two winters. In summer you can imagine being on holiday, whereas winter brings a different feel and the caravan can be far from static!

When it comes to caravan living, size really does matter. There are two main types of caravan: the static and the tourer. Given that you may be living in one of these for a couple of years, the vast majority of self-builders opt for the static caravan. This not only functions as your home but also doubles up as a site office, at least until you achieve a dry building. Printer, laptop and filing cabinet would all be found in a normal home office; but your site office will accumulate piles of invoices, rolls of plans, folders of official documents, sampler books and sample materials (not to mention cuddly toys if you have children!). A large static caravan is still a relatively small space to work and live in, compared with most homes. Do not lose sight of the word 'site'; it might be the only dry space to have discussions with Planners, Building Control Officers, Employees and Reps.

On the plus side and probably topping the list of incentives for caravan living is the financial consideration. The two years in the caravan saved around £20,000 in rent and lower Council Tax, taking into account set-up expenses. This is a significant amount, especially at the end of a build. Early living on site ensured that water, electricity, landline phone and broadband services were installed from the outset. Security was tight and deliveries could be received at any time. Additionally, work production was increased with a daily commute of under a minute!

Set against the advantages, you do have to factor in the extra commitment of locating, buying, delivering your caravan to site and probably selling it at the end. All this can be daunting but made a lot easier if you have any holiday caravan parks within a reasonable travelling distance. Such parks often replace a percentage of their stock at the end of the summer season. These static caravans will have been well used but also well maintained and probably be modern with competitive pricing. It is sometimes also possible to strike a deal for the delivery, jacking up and stabilising of the caravan. Alert! Your static caravan will probably be transported on the largest lorry to get to your site; one caravan delivery in a self-build TV series made a big impression on us when a corner of the caravan was badly damaged on entry to the site! Such problems can be minimised with some forward planning. We requested that our delivery driver ascertained the accessibility of our site prior to transportation. There was a fee for this which was to be absorbed in the overall delivery charge. Of course, it is imperative that the whole procedure of moving from site to site is insured, preferably by the person or company transporting the caravan. All went well with our delivery and the same driver was employed by our subsequent purchasers on our recommendation when our caravan was removed.

Reasonably new static caravans of about five to seven years of age, do come with significant creature comforts, including: toilet, shower and central heating. This is indeed what you would expect if you hired a caravan for a holiday. However, these caravans will generally not include a washing machine or tumble dryer. We constructed a small welfare shed to house these machines, together with the mandatory site toilet and basin.

Opting for a static caravan would generally mean putting furniture into storage. Over our three builds, we have progressed from a neighbour's garage, to an external shipping container and then finally a dedicated indoor storage facility. Increased sophistication equals greater cost. We would recommend avoiding the external metal shipping container; furniture and belongings often felt damp. Our most valuable possessions were placed with relatives and close friends. Do not assume that when you close the storage door, that's it until you move in! You will inevitably visit the storage facility from time to time. Careful loading with perhaps a diagram would be advised here.

The main negatives of caravan living in our experience are: that we couldn't entertain as we would wish, it could be cold and damp and was certainly cramped. Then there's mud, glorious mud! Our first caravan experience was with a young family. The fact that we repeated the exercise later in life suggests that the pros outweighed the cons; but oh those winter nights!

During both periods we made caravan living a bit more tolerable by joining a leisure club. This time round, we chose a hotel facility for a decent shower with a swim, along with a sauna and jacuzzi.

On one occasion, amidst the bubbles, a conversation was struck up with a couple of a similar age.

"Are you local?"

We responded with some pride: "Yes, we are self-building an oak frame house nearby and making caravan living more bearable!"

"That's a coincidence, we're self-building a bungalow locally, as well!"

There was so much to talk about and we lost all sense of time as we took it in turns to reactivate the bubbles. That is until we were interrupted by a rather indignant young lady, part of a hen party it seemed, suggesting that our time was up! We felt rather embarrassed at being evicted from a jacuzzi, having apparently and uncharacteristically shown little regard for others. It was though, a fortuitous meeting as we had stumbled across a very skilled 'chippy' with a lifetime of general building experience, who we have been able to employ regularly over the second half of the build. We are not tradespeople and have always recognised the importance of a skilled workforce.

Caravan living may not be for everyone. We coped well and the figure of around £20,000 saved, paid for a large proportion of our hardwood, double glazed windows. However, we can't imagine going on a caravan holiday anytime soon!

CHAPTER 7

Tooling Up

You will be using tools and equipment almost every day of the build if you choose the DIY route. The key is to purchase tools and equipment for frequent use and hire the remainder. Serial self-builders will have additional items of equipment, purchased for specific tasks. Bear in mind that tradespeople are expected to bring their own specialist tools.

The list of necessary daily tools and equipment for a self-build will vary with your build route (see Chapter 5). Build Route 'A', DIY and Sub-contractors will require more 'gear' than if a Main Contractor is engaged (Build Route 'D'). The following guidance is based on our Build Route 'A', DIY and Sub-contractors.

The power tools used on a regular basis included: a circular saw, impact driver, drill driver, jigsaw, mitre chop saw and percussion drill (2kg). These were mainly corded ie mains powered. Recognising improvements in quality over recent years, we also purchased a quality cordless kit of most of the above. This gave us more flexibility on site, reduced cabling and all pieces survived the build. Our existing table site saw was also extremely useful, given the softwood frame construction. The carpenter provided a planer/ thicknesser, router and nail gun as required.

Also proving essential were a tower scaffold, extending ladders, support props (acrows) and a cement mixer; all owned prior to this build. They can all be hired, but it is so much more convenient to have them to hand. A second, more lightweight scaffold tower was a useful additional purchase for the fixing of external cladding, in place of the more costly hire of fixed scaffolding for a second period. In addition, a dozen scaffold boards have had multiple uses from 'stretching' between the two scaffold towers, shuttering for the concrete slab, to a slate slide from roof to ground, saving much carrying time for the slaters.

Hired digger and dumper for heavy-duty work

We hired a five-tonne, tracked digger with a dumper and a plate compactor for the oak frame build. It was tempting to purchase a mini-digger; but we concluded that a larger machine was required for the 'cut and fill' process, involving the movement of a significant volume of soil and rock. The digger was hired again for the installation of the septic tank and drainage field. Avoiding the unpredictability of the weather, a week's digger hire is often preferable to the odd day or two at a greater hire rate as the cost differential is often minimal.

A 'Kubota' compact-size tractor with one-tonne trailer is evident in some of the photos. This was specifically purchased for a previous build for the removal of rock from an excavated barn. That site also had in excess of one acre of land and each time it has earned its keep once the building project had been completed. The front bucket has been an essential item of kit, enabling the efficient transportation of sand, block and stone around the site. The combination of tractor, bucket and trailer continues to give

**Our Kubota tractor with front bucket:
a real workhorse that has provided much family fun!**

great service, lately moving tonne-loads of horse manure from a neighbouring property for our self-sufficiency endeavours.

In addition to the audio level provided by the groundworker which could be individually operated, we purchased a laser level that rotated 360 degrees. This proved its worth when laying out the building on our sloping site with a round tower as a corner. Our slab had an error of 10 mm over 15 metres which apparently is very accurate!

Getting the job done with the appropriate tools can be rewarding and fun. You may purchase some equipment with the prospect of selling on at the end of the build; but in our experience, this tends not to happen. Our advice is to hire specialist tools as required and in the case of larger items such as diggers, take great care if you are using these powerful machines. In our case we generally limited our hands-on activity to the tractor, trailer and dumper, leaving more experienced personnel to handle the bigger 'toys'!

CHAPTER 8

Foundations

TV programmes such as 'Grand Designs' often show the digger breaking ground, following neat, fluorescent yellow marker lines defining the foundation trenches. What is not evident is the considerable amount of practical work that precedes this. In our case, we had to construct a track for heavy vehicle access. A service trench for water and phone was also dug and several sheds constructed, including a store for equipment and tools, a utility block housing the washing machine and freezer for caravan living and the all-important site WC facilities for workers. Bringing a static caravan to site, jacking it into position and connecting services, all takes time and money, before the real event begins.

The magical day finally arrives when all of the preparation work is behind you and your dream house build can start. What you have to absorb mentally and financially, is that for months the building works go down rather than up and this work, although vital, won't eventually be seen. Your site will become noisy, muddy and dangerous as large machines dig, transport and pile up soil and rock in ever-increasing quantities. The chosen way of dealing with our sloping site was, as previously described, a combination of cut and fill and stepped foundations. This was achieved competently by our regular builder/groundsman of some twenty years. We cannot over-emphasise the need for teamwork on a build, especially at the foundation stage.

The Structural Engineer's drawings required enlarged trenches in preparation for load-bearing oak posts. The foundation trenches were dug into shillet which is a fairly loose, but load-bearing rock. In the south east corner, when digging the tower foundations, clay was discovered, lots of it! We reached a depth of three metres before shillet reappeared. Once again, in building terms, what goes down

Collapsed foundation trench: only a shovel will do!

More shovelling: note Root Protection Zone
fencing in background

must come up. This phrase portrays the huge volume of block, stone and concrete necessary, merely to return to the surface level.

We dug our trenches in the wet Winter/Spring of 2017 and they frequently collapsed with the heavy rainfalls. This shillet had to be removed by hand. In all the work that we have ever tackled involving a mechanical digger, there were always plenty of opportunities to use a shovel. This seems to be the unwritten rule of building sites!

Stepped foundations require careful attention to the levels, often achieved with a series of 'pins'. The physical effort involved in filling the trenches to create footings can be greatly reduced by specifying a concrete lorry with a conveyor belt, enabling the

Tidied stepped foundation trenches prior to concreting: note levelling pins

Concrete lorry with conveyor belt reaching across
the site to fill trenches.

Block tower construction:
all this will be below finished ground.

concrete to be accurately placed into the trenches across the site. The site is then prepared for the slab, which is simply a layer of concrete over the entire footprint of the building. This is not just any old concrete; it's a sub-nuclear bunker-strength, 150 mm-thick concrete, together with reinforcing mesh, as specified by the Architect/Structural Engineer. You could probably have driven a tank over the slab once it had cured! Additional manpower will be needed to help with distribution and tamping the concrete level. Often, this whole flurry of activity is over by lunchtime and you can stand back to appreciate the footprint of your proposed new house. This is a significant stage of your build.

**Complete footprint in preparation for slab;
not a Roman villa excavation!**

Here is a cautionary concrete tale. Concrete companies/lorries note the arrival time on site. The lorries arrive and you have a reasonable amount of time to discharge the concrete. Exceed this time and you will pay for the overrun. There are two important aspects here: firstly, always give clear written instructions (typically by email) as to the time that the concrete is required, together with the time interval between deliveries and secondly, record the

Ready for Building Inspection before pouring foundation slab.

arrival time. On a former build, despite clear instructions to the Builders Merchants, we had one lorry discharging with three lorries waiting! It became clear that instructions had not been forwarded to the concrete supplier.

Building Regulations

A legal requirement of building a new house is compliance with the current Building Regulations. Our Architect submitted a comprehensive set of notes with drawings for approval by the Local Authority Building Control, who issued an inspection tick chart at the start of the build for Building Control visits. Alternatively, a private company can be instructed to carry out this inspection process. The Regulations cover everything from the tapes that you use to stick sheets of polythene together, width of windows on the first floor for evacuation purposes, spaces in front of toilets and even the heights of sockets and switches. It's a very long list, but specialist trades will be familiar with 'the Regs' applicable to their work and you will have time over the build to absorb the remainder.

Foundation slab, eight weeks from breaking ground

One of the initial visits is likely to be scheduled prior to pouring the concrete slab. These visits can be an opportunity to gain advice regarding the next stage of the build.

A misgiving about the Local Authority system is that, more often than not, a different officer is assigned for each inspection. We feel that it would be more beneficial for the self-builder to receive the same inspector, who would get to know you and the building as it progresses.

There will be a final 'completion' inspection. When achieved, it will confirm that your building meets current building standards and regulations. Our completion inspection in July 2020 was unusual in that it was conducted virtually. The Covid 19 epidemic prevented the site visit by the LA Inspector. The relevant documentation and certification were sent electronically. Certificates were required for electrics, heating, energy performance and windows, together with a range of photographs to demonstrate compliance. Our Assessment was successful and the Completion Certificate awarded; an important document which then enabled us to apply for our VAT refund and reduce our insurance premiums from a construction type to the usual household insurance.

'We cannot over-emphasise the need for teamwork on a build, especially at the foundation stage.'

The foundations and slab completed and inspected, we were 'out of the ground'. This is a major milestone in any build and a checkpoint for your budget control. We have previously mentioned that the tower was more difficult and costly than planned; but it fell within the contingency budget.

For us, this stage would be rapidly eclipsed by the arrival of our oak frame. You don't often get the surge of excitement on a build that we felt as the first timbers were erected. However, preceding the oak frame there was one more, extremely important preparation stage, omitted from more conventional builds; full scaffolding, both external and internal would be required prior to the erection of the oak frame.

CHAPTER 9

Scaffolding

If you are engaging a company to build your house, you will not be involved in the hire of scaffolding; it will appear and disappear at the appropriate times. However, if you are the Project Manager, then it is your responsibility to organise. In most, but not all circumstances, scaffolding will be hired from and erected by a scaffolding company. You basically work out your requirements and the anticipated duration of the hire, advisedly requesting at least three quotes. These quotes will consist of a fixed price over a stated period of time, followed by an overrun clause of so much per week beyond the initial hire time. It is the overrun, often due to circumstances beyond your control, which can adversely affect the overall scaffolding charge.

Conventionally-built houses of block and brick will not require scaffolding until the walls are up to first floor level. At this point, scaffolding will be delivered to create your first 'lift', that is a level where scaffolding planks are laid down for a walkway. You then continue up from this level to the eaves where a second lift is created to enable the roof to be constructed. This sequence avoids obstructing the building work.

Contrast the above description of scaffolding for a typical house construction with the complexity of our final email to our chosen scaffolding company. The Green Oak Company requested full scaffolding externally, including both lifts. An internal 'crash scaffold' was also required to be installed <u>after</u> the two major floor beams had been inserted. This would then be removed following the construction of the oak frame. Furthermore, there was the added complication of a stronger scaffold requirement, essential for support of the tower roof in the absence of walls!

A roller coaster of scaffolding prior to arrival of oak frame

Our chosen scaffolding company met these exacting requirements at a fair price. The confirmation email sent by us, together with acceptance of their quote, became the Contract which was successfully fulfilled by both parties.

'We thank you for your quote sent by email 16/02. The points below clarify the timetable requirements in order to finalise the quote.

- General purpose scaffold anticipated for a minimum of 6 months. We envisage an amendment to the general scaffold at the front of the house on the southern elevation, as the balcony is to be constructed after the main house build. Thus, the scaffold will continue straight across where the balcony will later be built.
- We trust that the attached drawing of the tower scaffolding sent recently by the Green Oak Carpentry Company meets with your expectations in providing your quote, inclusive of the 'round elevation'. A deck is planned

under the tower roof area, using scaffold ladder beams spanning from the normal scaffold either side, leaving the whole of the tower structure area clear below. The inside deck would be at a slightly higher level than the upper level of the ring scaffold – approximately 150mm below underside of plate is suggested. The tower roof ring plate would be assembled in blocking off this deck, along with the rest of the tower roof.

We would like to discuss the possibility of hiring this tower scaffold beyond the 6 months included in your quote. It is anticipated that this part would be required for around an additional 6 months. An alternative consideration would be to purchase this section of scaffold from your company.

- Please note that the internal crash scaffold, is required after the two major floor beams have been put in place during the erecting of the oak frame and would only be required for an estimated one week during construction of the oak frame.'

We strongly recommend that you use a bona fide company for scaffolding. This will satisfy your site insurance and will give you peace of mind, considering the amount of time that you and your sub-contractors will spend working at high levels.

Scaffolding Antics!

Throughout our three builds, we have been constantly reminded about how quickly you adapt to ladders and working at height. It becomes second nature and is necessary to get the job done. However, for most people, young or old, fit or unfit, running up and down ladders and being six metres above ground, on a narrow walkway with only a pole or two to protect you, is scary! When family or friends visit, don't be too disappointed when they don't share your enthusiasm to enjoy the view from on high! Do not force the issue as it is the coming down that causes trepidation. Also, unlike riding a bike, you need a period of adjustment; you do lose confidence. On each of our builds, Jan has been an extremely useful pair of hands on the second lift. However, it took her a little while to feel safe and to let go of that reassuring pole!

The tower roof was supported by quite a network of scaffolding which would remain in place until the tower walls were complete. This created problems when we tried to construct the serlio floor. These four large green oak beams, each weighing 100 kg plus, had to be hoisted up, pegged together and finally rotated in a very confined space. Several roof-supporting poles had to be 'relocated' in an adult version of pick-a-stick. This was one of the most awkward and nerve-racking moments of the entire build.

CHAPTER 10

The Arrival of the Oak Frame

A great deal of preparation was required before the oak frame arrived. When you commission an oak frame and receive the detailed drawings, you imagine this structure, freestanding in all its grandeur. In reality, you are faced with a roller-coaster type scaffolding framework, inside and out with the oak frame sandwiched in-between.

The day before the frame arrived, a huge crane was driven onto the site. This dwarfed the caravan and left just enough space to open the caravan door! The oak frame lorry was equally of mega-proportions, but failed to get onto site and so was discharged from the road below. This was achieved with precision, with each load carefully set down in the build order. A key part of the entire organisation was the fact that the carpenters who constructed the frame in Hampshire, would be erecting it in Cornwall.

How did the carpenters know the positioning of each piece of wood, bearing in mind that each pair of joints was individually handcrafted and therefore unique? Pencil and chalk marks would become illegible in a short period of time; so a system of chisel marks is used. There is no magic or luck in what skilled people do; it is simply experience, borne of good practice over an extended period of time and was exemplified by the oak frame construction.

Carpenter's tool marks

Huge crane for main event, the erecting of oak frame

Arrival of our oak frame house, all on one large lorry!

Precision unloading

This was clearly one of the defining moments of the build and apart from buying the plot, represented the largest invoice. We were about to appreciate the structure of our future house, that is if you could see the wood from the scaffold! From the outset, we were determined not to be a hindrance to the team. That attitude of keeping a low profile was definitely unrealistic, as we pointed the cameras excitedly in different directions with the craning and fixing of the timbers into position. The glory of the operation was enhanced by the beautiful April days that we experienced; it was hot and sunny and the young, efficient team readily accepted our offers of sun protection lotion.

**Project Manager's prerogative: symbolic fixing of peg.
Note internal scaffolding.**

The task was completed in just four days; perhaps in part, due to our ability to contribute! It was with considerable satisfaction that we were invited to secure a key peg in one of the central 'A' frames, complete with photographic evidence. We were also able to assist with a problem-solving exercise involving the positioning of the tower roof. It was certainly a real joy to be part of the process.

Wearing our Project Manager's hat, we requested that the oak roof of the tower, consisting of ring-beam and rafters, was installed at the same time as the main frame. We felt that it would have been difficult to build a vertical, spherical stone tower to the required degree of accuracy to receive the ring-beam and roof, at a later date. There is very little on the internet about integrating a round tower into a rectangular structure! We put a lot of thought into the practicalities. The key was that the east and south walls of the main rectangular house structure would be connected by the ring-beam, giving stability to that corner of the house. At this vital stage, we positioned ourselves to view this procedure. Just as the important securing of the ring-beam into the two vertical posts was to be achieved, the foreman playfully shouted: "Houston we have a problem!" There was apparently a discrepancy of 15 mm for the jointing of the ring-beam to one of the posts. Yes, it was a wind-up! He explained that he had deliberately left the joint 'proud' until final assembly. A saw, mallet and chisel created the perfect union.

It is worth noting the degree of craftsmanship involved in creating the tower roof. The oak ring-beam required a great deal of precision, cutting the curved circumference in segments from large timbers with accurate jointing. We view the 'boss', where the oak rafters from the ring-beam are secured at the top, as a work of art. All these components are assembled in the workshop before being dismantled for delivery to site. Ring-beam, rafters and boss are clearly visible inside the tower, as a constant reminder of the skill and dedication shown by the green oak craftsmen.

Later, with the ring-beam and roof sitting on reinforced scaffolding, it was a simple matter of dropping a plumb line from the centre of the roof to the slab floor, in order to scribe a floor circumference. This ensured accuracy in building a vertical, circular wall to within millimetres of the ring-beam, allowing for shrinkage of the oak.

Tower roof: ring-beam assembly

Oak rafters attached to boss

More oak rafters added: compare with workshop photo
Chapter 1 (metal podgers have been replaced with oak pegs).

Up, up and away!

"Houston, we have a problem!"
(Insertion of tower roof into oak frame.)

Possibly?

Of course!

The solution!

The oak frame is made up of tonnes of green oak with a high moisture content. It is heavy but easy to work and will slowly dry out and shrink. The oak will split as tensions are released within this process and it can even be noisy at times. It follows that if any part of the building butts up to an oak post or beam, gaps will appear over the years (see Chapter 12 on how to avoid these).

Oak frames for houses are designed in 'bays' and these average about four metres in width. Our house is 14 metres long, divided into three bays. Apparently, once you go beyond these dimensions, you need to seriously upgrade the engineering and therefore timber specifications.

The posts of our building sit directly on the reinforced concrete slab and are bolted to steel plates which are fixed into the concrete. Prior to delivery, the frames were laid out in the workshop and were fixed together using long metal pegs called podgers. These were then removed and replaced with seasoned oak pegs during the building process. They are very obvious in the building and are a reminder of a tried and tested, traditional technology.

Oak frame nearing completion with insertion of ridge timber.

Notes on Cleaning an Oak Frame

The oak frame arrives as sawn timber containing a variety of marks, blemishes and water stains. Water stains will increase until the building is weatherproof. There are three basic methods of cleaning the oak. Traditionally, sandblasting was used which is an extremely dirty and expensive method, carried out by a specialist company. The advantage is that the job is achieved in one hit. The remaining two processes are much more user-friendly for the self-builder and considerably cheaper. Sanding the oak is dusty and time-consuming. Gaining favour over recent years, is the use of oxalic acid, involving the dissolving of oxalic crystals in water to brush onto the oak which is left and then washed off. This process may need to be repeated several times, ideally before decorating.

The oak frame completed, we now had the defined spaces of our new home.

Perfect harmony

CHAPTER 11

■ ■ ■ ■ ■

Our Own Wood

Mobile sawmill on our second barn conversion project

Two large barn conversion projects preceded this oak frame build and on each of these we sourced timber in an unprocessed form. We bought beech 'in the round' at auction for our first barn conversion; that is wood from felled trees, planked and stacked for air seasoning. This was subsequently used for an extensive wood floor. The second barn conversion was on a farm which had its own woodland. In this case we needed green, unseasoned oak, to replace a variety of beams, studs and wallplates, together with external cladding. The farmer generously allowed two oak trees to be felled. Although not technically sustainable, we planted extensive beech hedging and an orchard on our site which compensated. We hired a mobile sawmill to reduce the two oaks to our lumber requirements.

Our one acre plot for our new oak-framed build came with a Tree Preservation Order (TPO) which was placed on it in around 1975. Specimen trees, including Austrian and Monterey Pines and a Sessile Oak were identified; but there were large spaces which were originally parts of the garden of the former Estate Manager's house, now a ruin. A condition of our Planning Permission stated that we were obliged to have a Tree Survey to establish the location of the protected trees. Root Protection Zones were identified and protective barrier fencing was erected during the construction process to comply with this Condition. Bats, newts and trees often strike fear into self-builders and developers; but if you adhere to the specialist advice, these environmental considerations can be worked through.

Repositioning planked ash using family labour!

The land came with two felled logs. We were informed that one of them, a beech was diseased. The other, an ash measuring over four metres long and half a metre wide, looked promising. It proved impossible to move, due to an access issue for large vehicles at the second entrance to the plot. This log couldn't be transported to a local sawmill; but we cast our minds back to a milling demonstration at the Royal Cornwall Show involving a chainsaw. A small portable rig was attached to the ash log and after five hours of almost continuous chainsawing, the specialist 'logger' produced two stacks of planked ash that were left to season for eighteen months. The wood was used predominantly for a bespoke staircase and also internal window sills, architrave and skirting.

A word of caution here. Firstly, there is no guarantee that a log will yield useful timber. It is currently uncertain as to whether ash dieback disease damages the internal structure or the appearance of the timber. Secondly, from a standing tree to a planed piece of timber requires many processes, all adding to the final cost of the finished wood. Woodyards do this at scale; individual efforts are more expensive. It was though, satisfying to use our own ash and it did prove economically viable.

Whilst our ash was home-produced, oak for oak frame buildings is invariably sourced from Normandy in France where it is grown in sustainable forests.

CHAPTER 12

Getting Dry

'May the roof above you never fall in,
And those gathered beneath it never fall out.'

(Irish origin)

Self-builders often talk about 'milestones'. The Planning Appeal, the completion of the foundation slab and the erection of the oak frame were particular milestones for us. Another eagerly awaited stage is that of being 'dry', as once the external fabric of the building is waterproof, work on the interior can start.

Modern oak frame houses do not look like their historical counterparts on the outside. You do not see much, if any exposed oak. This is nothing to do with style or fashion, rather the idea of avoiding 'cold bridging'. Oak that is exposed on the outside will radiate heat from the building. Building Regulations discourage this practice, unless windows are involved. Therefore, virtually all modern oak frames form the internal structure of the building. An external softwood frame is required to facilitate waterproofing, to insulate and also to act as strengthening bracing between the upright posts. The construction of this softwood frame, together with a roof, windows and external doors, create a waterproof structure, enabling internal building work to commence.

In our first building project, a barn conversion started in 1996, a cross-section of the wall from inside to outside would show just stone; no cavity, no waterproofing, no insulation and that's after conversion! Our modern oak-framed house couldn't be more different and it demonstrates how current Building Regulations have steered the building industry in the direction of energy efficiency and of course, comfort. This house does have a stone plinth on the outside, but behind it there are no less than nine separate layers, each with a specific function. These layers are described and explained, collectively creating the dry wall ready for fixing plasterboard before plastering and decorating.

1. Waterproof Membrane: Fixed to external part of the oak. All joins to be taped. Will form an entire covering of the building creating an airtight bubble.

2. 20 mm Spacers: These are attached to the oak beams and posts and will create 'shadows' that avoid plaster cracks when the oak shrinks.

3. Studs: 150 mm x 50 mm softwood timber fastened to the oak at 400 mm or 600 mm centres.

4. Insulation: Rigid 90 mm, placed between studs.

5. Plywood: 12 mm sheets fastened to studs. These provide the bracing/stability between the oak posts.

6. Insulation: Full sheets of rigid 50 mm; joints to be taped.

7. Breathable Membrane: This prevents moisture entering the wall, but allowing evaporation from within it.

8. Battens: 50 mm x 25 mm for attachment of Siberian larch cladding.

9. Cladding: Siberian larch

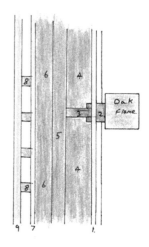

Typical Cross-section of our Oak Frame Wall

The first metre of the house, up to sill level, consists of a stone plinth and therefore instead of battens and Siberian larch cladding, a 50 mm-wide cavity stone wall was constructed. Construction of the tower was more conventional with two block walls forming an insulated cavity and external stonework.

Green waterproof membrane, studwork and plywood

First floor: addition of insulation and plywood

Base of stone wall, cavity and breathable
membrane with battens to receive cladding.

Tower wall construction: insulation and cavity
between soft block and concrete block

This softwood frame wall construction is well within the ability of the self-builder. However, there is an alternative; Structurally Insulated Panels (SIPS). This is a factory-based product and it will achieve a dry building in a fraction of the time, but at a price. You will need a crane to install.

Southern elevation slated with recycled Delabole slates.

The roof has a very similar profile to that of the walls, with a softwood frame created by the rafters, the insulation, breathable membrane, vertical (counter) batten, horizontal batten and finally slates. We applied the waterproof membrane at a later date, from the interior. This was purely a safety procedure to avoid standing on plastic sheets on the purlins and wallplates. Regular, recycled Delabole slates were chosen as the final course. These were more expensive and harder to source than new slate, but their grey, weathered appearance give an instant mellowed look which we find pleasing. Once again, SIPS panels could have replaced most of these individual stages in a fraction of the time, but at a much greater expense.

**Direct glazing of atrium with balcony attached:
note protective polythene around tower.**

The windows and external doors for our project were constructed in iroko hardwood by a local, specialist joinery company. These windows and doors have to meet quite tough regulations regarding insulation values and dimensions for evacuation from the first floor and for disabled access on the ground floor. Windows create the natural light of a building and that is why we designed the floor to ceiling, double-height atrium windows. We also placed most windows on the southerly aspect, to give not only a greater intensity of light but also for solar gain. It is crucial to the overall design of the building that windows and doors should be aesthetically pleasing.

With the completion of the walls, roof, windows and doors, the building is dry; another milestone. Work now starts on the interior of the building. Tasks for the self-builder could include laying floor joists to the first floor, together with installing chipboard/plywood floors to provide a safe platform for working on. We prepared the ground floor by laying a 120 mm rigid insulation followed by an underfloor heating (UFH) pipe network. This was covered in a 50 mm liquid screed that was pumped into the building, creating a self-levelling surface to the entire ground floor. The screed can be walked on the next day but takes a day per mm to completely cure. It was an excellent surface for laying the final 600 mm x 600 mm slate tiles.

Preparation for underfloor heating

Underfloor heating pipework in tower

Underfloor heating pipework in lounge and kitchen

Pouring 50 mm liquid screed

CHAPTER 13

First and Second Fixes

First fix plumbing

First and second fix are terms used in the trades to mainly describe the installation of plumbing, electrics and carpentry. The first fix requires these trades to position all the necessary wires, pipes and woodwork. The location of every sink, shower, toilet, bath, oven, socket, switch, phone, door etc. needs to be decided well in advance. This requires you to have an overview of how your building will look and function. That is a tall order and these trades should be patient with you, especially if it's your first build! It's a good idea to collect pictures of bathrooms, kitchens and lounges to give an indication of the style and look of the proposed interior. The trades will make suggestions based upon experience and their knowledge of the Building Regulations. 'Sparky', for instance will automatically wire for two-way switches for a second storey. The positioning of basin, toilet, bath and shower pipework in a family bathroom is decided at the first fix stage, not when the toilet is installed; so persuade the plumber to outline the fixtures in their proposed position on the floor to check if your plans work. Of course, all the wires and pipes will eventually be hidden by plasterboard before plastering. Mistakes often require intervention which at the very least will take time and money to rectify. Check installations carefully and frequently, perhaps at the end of the day when everyone has left. If you are not happy, say so diplomatically.

Just a hint on recycling; first and second fix will produce a fair quantity of offcuts such as bits of wire and odd bits of copper tube. Save everything, including all the pieces of discarded lead from the roofer's work. You will be very surprised at the scrapyard bonus paid at the end of the build!

Commencing second fix in family bathroom

Second fix involves the actual fittings: sanitaryware, lights, sockets, switches, doors etc. It is a long and yes, expensive list involving a great many decisions. Fortunately, there is often a gap between first and second fix when the majority of plasterboard is applied to the interior studs. Ensure that all studs are marked on floors and any ceiling beams in advance of sparky and chippy returning for second fix. Your house is turning into a home at last!

Notes on Contracts and Employing People

If you are employing a Principal Builder or a Building Company to build your house, they should formalise the arrangements in a written contract; basically, the house will be built according to the plans for a certain price. This type of contract will contain options regarding the specification of items, including the kitchen and bathroom fittings. Try to minimise the changes to the agreed plans, as an extra door or more light fittings will have an impact on the quote. These changes will need to be negotiated in advance to avoid difficulties afterwards.

Employing trades: chippy constructing studwork for rooms.

Most self-builders will not enter into formal contractual arrangements, simply because in order to be effective, legal jargon and perhaps a Solicitor may be required, involving extra costs. Our experience might be useful here. The oak frame, scaffolding, slating, joinery, glass and woodburner installations were priced for the job. Other employment on site was on an hourly rate basis. Some tradespeople charge per working day. Sometimes we used an email to express our wishes and to avoid ambiguity. The oak frame requirements for scaffolding were quite involved and therefore we summarised these in an email (Chapter 9) thereby creating a record that could be referred to in any dispute.

How it can all go wrong! (1)

Moving to a new area brings additional employment issues. You do not have a reservoir of proven local tradespeople. Where do you start? Before the onset of the build, we asked an unfamiliar worker to do some preparation work involving his digger. We requested that the work should start on a particular Monday at 8:00 am. We were living off site at the time. Unknown to us, our neighbour at the site was disturbed by the discharge of a noisy digger from a road trailer at 6:30 am, the previous weekend. The digger driver was confronted by the neighbour who was unaware of the clear arrangements that we had made to avoid such a situation! The digger driver's argument was logical, if rather inconsiderate; he wanted to start work promptly on the Monday morning, avoiding any traffic delays. Full marks for initiative; but there was a negative impact for us in forging our relationship with our new neighbour! If only the driver had bothered to communicate his intentions, a potentially nasty confrontation could have been avoided.

How it can all go wrong! (2)

When is a slate circle not a slate circle? In a previous barn conversion, we transformed a depressing, dark, dirty and damp blacksmith's work area into the main entrance of the barn. A three-metre, segmented slate circle within a square frame was selected for the floor. The end result created a stunning welcome space which we were keen to replicate in the tower, similarly as an entrance feature. We submitted a drawing, along with a photo of the proposed slate circle, to a reputable local company. They in turn produced a technical drawing and then outsourced the manufacture of the slate circle abroad.

A few months passed and the slate circle was duly delivered, unloaded and taken enthusiastically into the house. Yes, we still get excited when we know that we are creating something out of the ordinary. Each piece was carefully laid out around the 300 mm centre, in the lounge. That is until it became obvious that there was a serious mismatch between what was ordered and what we received. The company had not unpacked the circle from the imported pallet, so they were unaware of the error. We were looking at petals of a flower, rather than a segmented circle! It was possible to take an overhead photo from the atrium walkway and it certainly wasn't the specified slate circle. We forwarded the picture to the company. These circles are not cheap and Jan and I looked at each other thinking: "Is this another battle?"

How it can all go wrong: slate petals!

The inserted slate tower floor, as designed!

The company was as perplexed as us; the supplied slate circle bore little resemblance to the submitted drawings. This reputable company apologised immediately, indicating that they would produce the slate circle themselves and we are very pleased with the final result. Two considerations to mention here: always keep a copy of any bespoke drawings in the event of a dispute and secondly, is there a use for a petalled, slate circle?

Plastering kitchen

We were fortunate in having good finishers for our oak frame build. It is worth reiterating the notion of sequencing here and the way that tradespeople typically organise their work to counter delays that frequently occur with a project. Your project is probably one of several scheduled jobs. Imagine if you receive a phone call from your window firm informing you of a two-week delay in the installation of your joinery. The impact is that you will not then be 'dry' for the fitting of plasterboard, perhaps scheduled for the following week. The scheduled tradespeople will rearrange their other work to avoid a slack period. This may, for example, be for a four-week period, in which case your original two-week delay has now extended into a month. That spreadsheet schedule is becoming fiction not fact! Yes, if your build extends beyond your anticipated duration, there are likely to be extra costs in for example, scaffolding hire, site insurance and perhaps toilet hire.

Sequencing and Stage Mortgage Payments

We have not entered into the sourcing of finance for your self-build. However, while we are discussing delays and sequencing, it may be worth mentioning the possible implications of the Staged Payment Mortgage. It is customary that if you purchase a house, you acquire a mortgage for the price of that house, minus the deposit. This is impractical for the self-builder and the mortgage provider, because at the start there is no house! Thus, a scheme has been devised whereby your mortgage payments are given in staged instalments as the building progresses. These payments could be in advance, but invariably they are in arrears, meaning that payment is made on completion of a particular stage. Typical stages could be the foundations, eaves level, watertight roof, plastered internal walls and completion. Now, if for any reason a stage is delayed, payment will be withheld. Keeping to a sensible schedule in these circumstances is essential, otherwise your project will stop-start, depending on finance.

Protective green polythene on tower enabled installation of large serlio floor timbers.

If you are the Project Manager, thinking outside the box could mitigate some of the sequencing issues. In the case of delayed windows, the installation of temporary polythene protection in one part of a building, could enable internal work to continue. In our case, we wrapped the tower scaffolding in heavy-duty polythene which allowed work to continue in all weathers, eventually creating a dry house. Good decision-making and problem-solving are key to maintaining the momentum of a build.

And Finally ....

An Englishman and his wife in Provence, France were converting a building and experiencing difficulty in getting the various trades to finish their jobs before Christmas; that is until his wife had a clever idea. Why not invite the tradesmen and their wives to a party? She thought that the wives would be curious about their husbands' work. However, more importantly, no wife would want her husband to be guilty of not finishing; it would be embarrassing. The ploy worked and all the work was completed before the party. We wonder if such a devious tactic would work in the UK?

Assuming that you are not planning to do all the work yourself, take great care in employing recommended tradespeople. Make clear arrangements with careful instructions regarding timeframe and payment terms, ideally formalised in that all important email or letter.

CHAPTER 14

The Moving in Debate

Self-builders could be either renting a property, living on site in a caravan or living in their existing home which they typically need to sell to fund the build. The caravan gives you a degree of choice over the moving in date; the other two options generally come with either contractual financial obligations in the case of renting or the unpredictability of a house sale.

The magazines and TV programmes show the entire time range of moving in options from turnkey finished to camping in a shell of a house. Our experience is useful here in that it demonstrates how circumstances can change a carefully organised plan.

No comment!

We were living in the caravan on site, having survived two winters. The plan was to sell the comparatively modern, 28-feet static caravan before the next winter. Sensibly, we anticipated that it might take many months to find a buyer. The caravan was advertised. We should add that at this time, the house was without a kitchen, hot water, upstairs electricity and had yet to be plastered. It was little more than a shell. To our great surprise and (perhaps) delight, we found a buyer in days; another self-build couple. The move into the house was imminent and not the planned choice suggested above!

The benefits of moving in were: that we had more space, we were able to retrieve our possessions from self-storage and our build capital was replenished. This is a short list; but we did not regret moving in and we found that living with the space inspired further creative design. The negatives are all too obvious: living within a partially constructed building with the inevitable noise, dirt, dust and lack of privacy. These discomforts were all outweighed by the pleasure of living in our new home. Of course, the ideal is to move in when finished; but each self-builder has a unique situation which can change over time. In our opinion, the ability to adapt to circumstances, is one of the key attributes of a self-builder.

A static caravan for a self-build project generally requires Planning Permission and this triggers a Council Tax Assessment, which for us was set in the lowest Band 'A'. About one month after the caravan left the site, we had a visitor from the Council, noting the disappearance of the caravan and wanting to reassess our circumstances. We anticipated continuing to pay the Band 'A' tariff until the conclusion of the build, pointing out that the house had fewer facilities than the caravan at that particular point in time; the kitchen had yet to be installed, there was no hot water and no electrics upstairs. Months went by before a Rateable Valuation Officer attended for an intermediate assessment. He strongly suggested that the limited facilities should ensure a relatively low, temporary banding. Further months went by before notification and to our dismay, we had been assigned the much higher banding attributable to the finished house and it was to be backdated to the time of first habitation! We protested at this decision and tried to ascertain whether the Council could claim rates on a building that fell well below the standards and facilities for a legal rental. Eventually, after careful consideration by two Valuation Managers, it was made very clear to us that Rates are charged on the value of the plot, together with the worth of the building at its degree of existing development, irrespective of the facilities available. The long delays in the assessment process had caused the accumulation of an expensive, retrospective bill! Is this a good argument for not moving in too soon?

It may be selective editing that portrays typical TV self-builds as being tackled by a husband and wife or partners. These shows often perpetuate stereotypical roles with the man spending his days mixing concrete, running up and down ladders, cutting up insulation and generally assisting the trades on site. His work is portrayed as practical, productive, sociable and even warm. In contrast, his wife/partner is often filmed in a cold, damp caravan, spending their day worrying about the deluge of invoices, the mud, the washing and other daily chores.

The programmes frequently show a premature move into the unfinished house in order to save money. The shell of a house remains his place of work, whilst the wife/partner typically has a different perception; it is home to the family (not to mention the new additions!). It is constantly trashed by noise, dirt and dust from eight in the morning to five or six in the evening, continuing for months or even years. Privacy has all but disappeared as a variety of workers, come and go during the day.

At last, the house is finished and the now smartly dressed couple are directly asked if they would contemplate another build. The anticipated affirmative often expressed by the man with a denial from his partner, are testament to the individual journey each have experienced; one partner portrayed as practically creating and constructing the house and the other concerned more with dwindling finances and domesticity in difficult circumstances. On reflection, the majority of these programmes exhibit traditional gender roles; although increasingly, role reversals are becoming evident, particularly in Project Management at a time when more women are taking up Building Apprenticeships. Frequently, the family appear as painters and decorators as the project concludes and finances become stretched.

Asking the question: "Would you do it again?" to programme participants immediately at the end of a build, probably gives a negative, knee-jerk response. The fact that we have been driven to instigate three substantial projects over the last twenty-five years, indicates that overall the experience has remained a positive adventure for us. We are extremely proud of having created over 1,000 square metres of buildings in Cornwall with varying functions. We have now drawn the line at further developments, not because we didn't enjoy our experiences, but as we approach 70 years of age, we are seriously considering retirement!

CHAPTER 15

Energy

Global warming is occurring and the UK Government is determined that new housing will not exacerbate the issue. In Part L of the Building Regulations, there is a great deal of prescription concerning the energy efficiency of your new house including: the windows, walls, floors, roof, types of light-fittings and bulbs and airtightness of the building. Mandatory minimum standards are useful; but most self-builders go beyond these in their desire to future proof their proposed longstanding home. Your Architect will talk about Standard Assessment Procedures (SAPS) which is the overall indicator of the energy efficiency of your house. The higher the efficiency you opt for, the greater the initial financial outlay will be for window specifications, wall, floor and ceiling insulation and methods of heating the building. However, in the long-term, your heating and electricity bills will be correspondingly much lower and your carbon footprint reduced.

On a sunny January day with no heating, the internal temperature of our home reached 22 degrees Centigrade, remaining above 20 degrees C for much of the evening. Our building is very eco-friendly and this starts from its favoured position on a south-facing slope. The house is designed to capture the sun's energy all year round, for free! The majority of our windows, including a four-metre high atrium are on this south elevation, all helping in this solar gain. The external balcony provides shade in the summer months to prevent overheating. This solar energy is stored in the slate floor and brick fireplace and is retained in the building due to the high degree of 140 mm 'wraparound' insulation in the walls and roof. Double glazed windows also help to retain this heat and in addition, the entire building is wrapped internally within a polythene bubble, preventing virtually all air leakage to the outside. This airtightness is rigorously tested (see notes on Air Pressure Test at the end of the chapter) as part of your building's

Energy Performance Certificate (EPC). Thus, we have a snug building, provided by passive elements, especially insulation which the self-builder is quite capable of installing.

Going green: air source heat pump installed

**'Stylish woodburner .... cheery, aesthetic
focal point in the lounge.'**

What about the cold, cloudy days in winter? We have installed underfloor heating (UFH) to the entire ground floor. This is a water-filled pipe network, covered in a 50 mm liquid concrete screed. There are four separate zones, each with its regulating thermostat. Initially, we were intending to heat this system with a combination of an oil-fired boiler and a woodburning stove with back boiler in the open-plan lounge. In plumbing terms, this was combining an open and closed heating system. We decided to simplify this complicated arrangement to a woodburner in the lounge and to 'go green', replacing the 'dirty' technology of an oil-fired boiler with an air source heat pump (ASHP). In essence, this is a machine outside the building that extracts energy from the air and stores it in a water tank in the plant room. We were partly influenced here by a Government scheme, the Renewable Heat Incentive (RHI). The initial financial outlay for the ASHP was approximately £3,000 above that of the oil-fired boiler; but we receive a quarterly payback over a seven-year period which amounts to a substantial contribution towards our capital cost. The ASHP provides all our hot water, including the UFH. We did install a very efficient, stylish woodburner which is a cheery, aesthetic focal point in the lounge.

Many people install photovoltaic cells (PVs) on the roof to provide the electricity to run the heat pump. We did not want to adversely affect the mellow look of our recycled Delabole slates and so opted instead for an electricity provider with 'green' renewable credentials. The oak frame, together with the ASHP reduces our carbon footprint. This is currently our contribution to the post-Covid green industrial revolution.

Electrical components are part of the energy brief of a building. The efficiency of light bulbs has accelerated over the years from the old incandescent, through to compact fluorescent and the current LEDs which have become universal in new-builds. Similarly, appliances have become more energy saving and smart meters also reduce energy consumption in the home.

The total components of all the Standard Assessment Procedures will contribute towards your Energy Performance Certificate. This summary, including the passive elements of insulation and aspect, through to ASHP and a successful Air Pressure test, amount to a total energy worthiness of your building.

These energy requirements for a new home are mandatory with the exception of the ASHP. From 2025, at the time of going to press, fossil fuel appliances (coal, oil and gas boilers) will be prohibited in all new developments. These standards are high and expensive. They are designed to drive up energy efficiencies in the nation's existing housing stock, thereby creating more comfortable homes with smaller carbon footprints.

Two Important Notes on Trends

1. MHRV: Many self-builders are installing Mechanical Heat Recovery Ventilation systems. These machines recover heat from rooms such as bathrooms and kitchens, rather than expelling it in the usual way to the outside. They also filter air within the building.
2. Overheating: 'In our temperate climate, and to comply with Building Regs, we tend to focus on heat retention ..... and often overlook the even bigger problem of overheating.' (David Hilton, 'Homebuilding and Renovating', August 2018 page 163.)

When we were planning our oak frame, an external oak balcony was carefully considered for the south elevation. It would enhance the appearance of the house and offer wonderful views over the valley as well as providing some much-needed shade for the lounge. We were initially concerned about the restriction of light as well as the inevitable stretching of our budget. Reassurance came from a fortuitous consultation at one of the 'Homebuilding and Renovating' trade shows held regularly around the country. We decided to take advantage of the free architectural consultation, asking a simple question: "Should we build the balcony?"

Internal atrium walkway looking out to external balcony

The answer was a resounding: "Yes!" This was partly based on aesthetics, it looked good; but it was mainly due to the energy equation of the building. The balcony would prevent overheating in a warm house. If global warming continues and thermally efficient homes become standard, will the new growth industry be air conditioning units?

Air Pressure Test

On several occasions, we have referred to the airtight bubble that is created within the building, achieved by joining up large sheets of polythene with extremely strong tape. This bubble covers the entire structure, apart from the windows and doors. Great care must be taken to seal window and door frames before testing. Skilful repairs using plenty of tape are required where soil and water pipes and electrical wires penetrate this skin. The Air Pressure Test is for new-builds where the airtight bubble is feasible. Renovations, restorations and refurbishments do not officially require this level of airtightness, simply because it would be impractical.

Airtightness in action: sealing around windows

Retaining the heat generated within the building will significantly reduce the energy consumed. The Air Pressure Test is conducted to calculate air leakage. On the day of the test, all vents including extractors are sealed. An airtight frame is then placed over a key external door and a fan literally starts sucking the air out of your building, creating a small vacuum. Even the best of modern buildings will have incoming drafts.* A monitor calculates the level of leakage. It is often stated that as a result of the high degree of airtightness of a modern house, space heating is unnecessary. Most self-builders err on the side of caution by installing some UFH and perhaps a woodburner. We have not regretted our decision to install both of these.

---

* Our building passed the Air Pressure Test, as required by our SAPs. Once completed, we reopened our trickle vents above all windows to give natural ventilation.

CHAPTER 16

Lockdowns 2020-21

Finished stairs in factory, awaiting delivery following Lockdown.

2020 was a difficult year in which to construct or attempt to complete a building. The Covid 19 pandemic would create havoc with people's lives, their jobs and the economy. On 23rd March 2020, the Government announced a total lockdown of the entire country, restricting movement, employment, entertainment etc. This would not be eased until the summer months. Of course, if you are self-building, you were able to continue, providing that you could obtain materials. We have included a photo indicating a forlorn image of our bespoke ash stairs in a local factory. They were made and 'good-to-go', but could not be delivered because of the lockdown restrictions. We eventually received the stairs at the beginning of June.

Lockdown landscaping: gabion cages

Lawn creation: initial stage

Progress with levelling

The end product: a seeded lawn

Sequencing has been mentioned before. Without the stairs, we couldn't order the glass for the balustrade and we couldn't install the bank of light switches in the lounge, all of which delayed our completion and involved extending our construction site insurance at significant cost. (Toilet paper and flour were in very short supply; but this did not really impact on our build!)

While waiting for the stairs, we turned our attention to landscaping, including the restoration of a former entrance and levelling the sloping site for a lawn. The surplus material removed from the entrance was deposited on the slope to the east of the house. Gabions had been constructed to retain this material. These cages absorb the pressure of the made-up ground. The outer gabion wall on view was faced with stone, just as if building a dry stone wall and backfilled with tonnes and tonnes of rejected stone that had originally been used to fill the cavity between two facing walls in the ruin. Creating the gabion wall took weeks. We were proud of our efforts. A digger levelled the site and by late June we had sown the lawn. Without Lockdown, this work might have been delayed until the autumn or even the following spring.

We discovered once before during a barn conversion, that levelling a sloping site can really enhance the appearance and significance of a building as well as creating a flat piece of land. Kevin McCloud of 'Grand Designs' fame often concludes his programmes by describing the buildings as being 'rooted in the landscape'.

Finally, lockdown restrictions were lifted in June and our stairs were delivered and installed. The balustrade was measured for glass and was promptly fitted a few weeks later. All that was needed were a few finishing touches, including electrical testing for the required commissioning certification. You are issued with a wodge of paperwork to forward to Building Control, indicating that your building is wired up safely and complies with the Building Regulations.

Once these final jobs had been 'done and dusted', we then implemented the 'Completion' process, the final major milestone

End of first Lockdown 2020:
stairs, balustrade and glass installed.

of our build. Completion is the process whereby the Building Control Officer, representing the Local Authority, inspects your property for the final time and electrical, heating, EPC and SAPs certificates are ratified. The visit is a somewhat nervous occasion because, if for any reason you are deemed not to have complied with a Regulation, the Inspector can insist on the work being carried out before issuing the Completion Certificate. This certificate is the passport to changing the insurance status from building site to a domestic house rate and is a formal requirement for a VAT* refund for self-builders. Completion is therefore very important.

We contacted the Building Control Office in July, requesting the all-important Completion inspection, only to be told that these

---

* There are exceptions to the Completion Certificate as a means of applying for the VAT refund, but this would be the usual route.

Completion achieved remotely:
first floor window opening for evacuation.

Completion Assessment: kitchen heat alarm

Completion Assessment: en-suite extractor

Completion Assessment:
disabled access over threshold

visits were not taking place due to the Covid 19 pandemic. Ugh! It was explained though, that this could be achieved virtually. What a relief! The Building Control Officer gave a list of items and areas that we should video or photograph within the building as evidence of compliance. The list concentrated on disability access, the ability to evacuate the building from the first floor, means of air extraction and alarm systems. These were reviewed by the Building Control Officer and following a short phone call on a Saturday morning, a Completion Certificate was downloaded.

Lockdown 2021: Experimental Archaeology

Over the past six years of owning the site and commencing months before any building work, we laboriously dug inside and outside the ruin, creating huge piles of stone of varying quality which would all eventually be used throughout the site for various purposes. A great slab of concrete blocks had been unearthed measuring several metres in length, three blocks wide and two blocks deep, all covered in render. The tractor and mini-digger failed to shift this heavy structure and drilling holes to weaken it, made no impact. Hold that thought!

Chris has always enjoyed reading about Roman history and brought to mind Hannibal and his elephants crossing the Alps in 218 BC in order to attack Rome! Whilst ascending the passes was manageable, descending was much more difficult. To help the descent, Hannibal created fires on the tracks and then poured wine on the hot rocks to cool them down. The ensuing contraction broke up the track, making an easier descent.

Back to the plot; surely it was worth a try, perhaps using water rather than wine! A great pile of twigs was placed around and on the slab and after months of wet weather, four consecutive dry days appeared. It was a very hot fire and with some reluctance, two large buckets of cold water were discharged and everything disappeared in a cloud of steam. Slowly this cleared. Had our experimental archaeology succeeded? Faint cracks along the entire length of the slab appeared; thank you Hannibal! We must point out that several smaller fires were necessary to crack the lower layer.

Experimental Archaeology has been taken to a whole new level in France, where at Guedelon, a Mediaeval castle is being constructed, respecting the same working conditions as a 13th century construction site, without electricity or mechanical machinery, '....... allowing, as it does, insights into lost skills and techniques'. If you enjoy reading our book, then reading about Guedelon is sure to inspire you (see Appendix 3: Further Reading).

The first Lockdown in 2020, was a period of particular disruption and uncertainty which affected timing and finance; but as always, we steadily worked through it and achieved our goal. In Lockdown 2021, our site continued to present challenges and interest .... with no wine wasted!

CHAPTER 17

■ ■ ■ ■ ■

Those Telly-builds

If you are contemplating building your own home, the chances are that you were not inspired by visiting a building site, but by the many and various reality build programmes such as 'Grand Designs' and 'Building the Dream'. They are often on at prime times and then there are the repeats. How realistic, honest and responsible are these programmes, given their potential influence to encourage others?

The film companies are there at the start of a build; but unlike a film, there is no set script, no story boards and the final scene is unwritten. No doubt, not all the programmes make the small screen; cynically, we get to see the ones that make 'good telly'. This is not to say that all the builds are successful. We give the companies credit here for balance. Many at this stage are like show homes, complete with the bay trees at the front entrance. If the building project is unfinished, it merely gives a golden opportunity for the 'Revisit'. These can be informative. You see a home and garden that is lived in.

If you invite the cameras in, you achieve a visual record of the build, advice and perhaps recognition of an exemplary home. However, do these advantages compensate for the inevitable disruption, increased time pressures, possible temptation to upgrade and exposure to criticism if advice is not heeded? Searching questions throughout the build regarding the budget and your financial position appear intrusive. Finally, you have to consider that your home, your personality and possible failures could be regularly broadcast as repeats.

One thing that has always perplexed us is furniture. Why is it, when during the entire build, money may have been such a scarce commodity, the new home is adorned with fabulous new furniture? Another conundrum, is the simplistic attitude towards valuations in the final scene:

"Do you know what it is worth?"
"We had an Estate Agent around last week ...."

You would never rely upon one valuation. Are these values inflated as if to reward the self-builder? Also, there is sometimes a world of difference between a valuation of a property and the price accepted for a sale. We often wonder whether the figures typically volunteered by the self-builders are aspirational rather than based on a rigorous market appraisal.

The film production companies condense a year or more of a build into a one-hour show, incorporating four or five visits. There is a considerable amount of editing which, more often than not, concentrates on decisions of design or disruptions of the weather, rather than on more practical areas, such as cavity wall construction, type of insulation and the heat source. The benchmark of these shows, 'Grand Designs', presented by Kevin McCloud, has over the years included new-builds, Listed and non-Listed renovations and conversions, derelict sites and extensions. Such programmes have demonstrated innovative designs and technologies. These designs can sometimes cling to a cliff or be shoe-horned into a tiny urban space with build budgets running into millions. Kevin McCloud is very honest about inadequate budgets, unrealistic time frames and not employing enough professionals. Programmes get extremely interesting when the Architect is also the owner. In these situations, any significant changes in design (because they can!) can result in overruns in budget and time. We only highlight this because self-builders often look to Architects to avoid these situations!

Windows! If you order triple glazed, self-cleaning, thermal-efficient windows from some factory in Europe, they will invariably be late, according to the programmes. We are then into our old friend, sequencing. It is true that if you order double glazed windows from a local supplier, this could also happen; but at least communications would be potentially easier. We have always ordered our windows from local companies and they have been of excellent quality and on time. Further, the firms have indicated genuine gratitude for the order. The difficulty experienced on many builds is that all window openings have to be formed and subsequently precisely measured*. There is an inevitable interval between measuring and installing the windows, during which time the building is not dry. This interval can often be translated into: "They're late!" when in fact a company may be working flat out to complete your order.

Charlie Luxton's 'Building the Dream' is much more basic self-build territory than 'Grand Designs'. He too is quite candid about time and money while also praising the achievements of the self-builders. Charlie often arranges visits to completed projects which is a real help in the decision-making process; but why does every kitchen need an island? Related to this visit idea, oak frame companies sometimes offer an overnight or a weekend stay in a show home as a kind of 'test drive'.

A worrying element in these shows is the financial failure of businesses supplying goods and services. The impact of contractors and suppliers of large budget items, such as heating systems, kitchens or wood frames, 'going bust' can be considerable in time and money. Furthermore, it is often difficult to engage another contractor to continue the work seamlessly. There will inevitably be a time delay impacting on once again, sequencing. Expensive items and installations such as an oak frame, an ASHP or windows, will probably require instalment payments to the manufacturers. These will be unavoidable; but due diligence in researching the company should give some peace of mind. Avoid disproportionately large

---

* Leaving the measuring to the window company is always to be recommended. They know the tolerances of the materials and take responsibility for any poor fit.

upfront payments as far as possible; but work with local companies in a responsible way ensuring prompt payment when it is due.

Emotions! We think it is impossible to spend the amount of money, time and energy required on a build, without feeling emotional about the journey or the resulting building. With older buildings there is also the added responsibility of a sympathetic treatment. Emotional investment exists from the inception of the dream and frequently increases with the pressures of the build. It is often at the end of a programme that the skilled presenter creates a reflective mood of what has been achieved, leading to the inevitable: "Give me a moment!" The congratulatory comments at the end of a build are absorbed with gratitude, especially from seasoned presenters. Teachers know the value of praise!

These telly-builds are inspirational and demonstrate what can be achieved. They also broadcast projects that don't succeed to create a balanced viewing. Think twice though before sharing your build with the world and definitely don't write a book!

CHAPTER 18

Weather

British people have a habit of talking about the weather, mainly because it can vary considerably within a day, let alone the seasons. Self-builders though, are not in a queue or on a commuter train making polite conversation; our job often involves the great outdoors and the elements.

The vast majority of telly-builds have one thing in common; interruptions because of the great British weather. Most self-builds would take at least a year and therefore would experience all four seasons. We broke ground in early February, a wet February; the site was muddy and slippery and great care was necessary in moving around, both on foot and with the heavy machinery. The rainfall saturated the foundation trenches which lead to some

Even in Cornwall, weather conditions can halt all external work.

collapse, especially on the corners. A great deal of time was spent clearing this material by hand, since a mechanical digger would have only exacerbated the problem.

The oak frame arrived in April, during a particularly hot, sunny week which meant supplying the oak frame team with suncream. On a building site, both severe heat and cold impact on productivity. Working in the rain for any length of time, even wearing waterproofs, will chill and slow you down. The screed to cover the UFH arrived during a cold snap, the following February when we endured 'The Beast from the East'. The 50 mm liquid screed covering required a minimum temperature of 5 degrees Centigrade to cure; but the external temperature was well below this when it was poured. We resorted to electrical space heaters in the absence of any domestic installations. The snow scene shows weather conditions which halted all external work and even stopped deliveries. You cannot do stone or brickwork in low temperatures or in the wet. It is frustrating paying for downtime resulting from inclement weather.

Storm damage requiring remedial work.

Sometimes on a build, a particular job cannot be concluded due to perhaps, poor light, lack of materials, tiredness or merely over-confident planning! On one occasion, the final insulation cladding, large 50 mm rigid sheets 2.4 x 1.2 metre were tacked to the rear of the building using 100 mm nails and strong tape. Battens were due to secure this the following day, in preparation for the final wood cladding. However, overnight a strong southerly wind developed, 'sucking' the insulation from the north elevation. There wasn't a big impact financially, perhaps just some additional tape, but it was frustrating to have to repeat the work, before finally applying the battens!

Slaters completing tower roof: a hardy breed!

It is not only working in difficult conditions; the weather can also impact on the materials that you are using. Softwood timber left exposed to the sun will warp. Blocks and bricks can become saturated and difficult to lay. Sand piles have a tendency to creep during wet weather; although by far the biggest irritation must be cats on uncovered piles!

We had the slater and his labourer working on the roof on a very windy day. Chris overheard the roofer instructing the labourer to sit down. Concerned, he suggested that the work could wait; but the roofers stated that they had seen worse! It was in fact so windy that Jan's planned return flight from Stansted to Cornwall, following a few days visiting family, had been cancelled. She was bussed to a hotel near Gatwick for a flight the following day. Jan arrived home a day late, having experimented with flying rather than driving to Essex to minimise travelling time!

There is a saying that there is no such thing as the wrong weather, just the wrong clothing; but know when to call it a day. We always tried to ensure that there was enough internal work where possible for those difficult days.

CHAPTER 19

The VAT Question

When you purchase a house, new or old in the UK you do not pay VAT. Similarly, if you build a house, you should not pay VAT. However, the current system is retrospective; you pay the VAT and then at the end of the build, you make a once only claim.

There are interesting mechanisms within the scheme. If you have a product supplied and fitted, for instance our oak frame or our windows, you get a zero rating, that is without a VAT charge. You need to provide evidence to the supplier that it is a new-build, such as a Planning Permission letter. You cannot claim for professional services such as architects, structural engineers or quantity surveyors. In our view, this seems rather unfair to the self-builder who characteristically builds a unique house, requiring distinctive professional services. Further, you cannot claim for consumables such as sandpaper, white spirit or cleaning materials. It would be very difficult to build a house without such items!

What can you claim VAT back on? It boils down to material items that are in the construction of the house or grounds. There are even guidelines detailing the number of fixings required for a 'fitted' wardrobe. Indeed, what is classified and acceptable as 'built-in' in the VAT documentation is debatable, with ovens and hobs deemed unacceptable while a cooking range is, providing it also supplies hot water. Surprisingly, if a swimming pool is included in your Planning Permission, the VAT refund can be claimed!

What is the procedure for claiming back VAT? You obtain a VAT Refund Pack from the VAT Office. All claims must be supported with valid invoices containing your name and address. More often than not, you will have to ask suppliers to include these details.

These invoices are then entered onto the supplied recording sheets. We had over 600 valid invoices for our oak frame build, so it is important to keep up to date with the entries. It is also prudent to chase late invoices; an overlooked £100 invoice is a £20 VAT claim.

A positive side to your VAT records is that they are a very useful reference, especially on pricing. Subtle price increases can be discussed with builder's merchants if you have the evidence to hand. A further benefit of keeping up to date with the recording of invoices is the cumulative totals at the bottom of each page; that is what the Government owes you!

Take great care with credit notes. This is when you have purchased a product, entered the VAT on the sheet and then returned or exchanged the item. Technically, you would be claiming for VAT that you were not charged for. A credit note provided by the supplier is issued which is entered in red and deducted from the VAT total. If we were VAT Officers, we would be very suspicious if we did not see red entries on these sheets!

Having sent off your VAT claim, be patient. The money due, typically between £10,000 and £30,000, is often perceived to be a great bonus at the end of the build; if only! Many self-builders would have already accounted for this refund in order to finish their builds. In stark contrast to the self-build VAT scheme, businesses send quarterly financial returns to HMRC. Why can't self-builders enjoy a similar scheme instead of waiting, sometimes years, for money that is lawfully theirs?

'Dunroaming', 'Rose Cottage' or 'Apple Tree House' might well be your desired house name. However, we would advise that whatever your registered site address is, you maintain this throughout the entire build. VAT invoices must indicate a consistent site address. It is not until the VAT claim has been successfully concluded that you can think about changes. On reflection, by far the best idea is to instigate a permanent address from the beginning.

We applied for our VAT refund on 7th July 2020. The HMRC information indicates that refunds should be achieved in approximately six weeks. However, due to a Covid 19 covering clause, it was not until 31st December 2020 that the refund appeared in our account.

Further, one of our larger invoices failed to have the Company VAT Registration number on the paperwork. Well-spotted VAT staff! We were given the opportunity to reclaim this and it finally arrived on 23rd February 2021.

CHAPTER 20

Light Bulb Moments

If you've ever had a discussion with a self-builder or have self-built yourself, there is one inescapable fact; the build is as much about the self-builders as it is about the building. This book, this oak frame build, is about us. Over the last twenty-five years, we have achieved three significant building projects, the result of serious research and decision-making. There are though, three light bulb moments over a longer period, any one of which could have redirected our entire lives and builds.

We often wonder: 'What if ....?'

Imagine King Harold side-stepping the arrow at the Battle of Hastings in 1066 and the English had won the day? The impact would have been more far-reaching than no Norman castles! On a more lowly, more personal level, we had three: 'What if ....?' moments that have defined our direction of travel in life. What if our Teaching job-share proposal had been accepted? What if the amalgamation of our Children's Nursery with two large local primary schools had succeeded? Finally: What if building on an old farmhouse plot had achieved approval from the Planners? If any of the above had come to fruition, the current oak frame build would have been highly unlikely. What were the consequences of those light bulb moments?

Job-share

In 1986, Jan was a Year 5 Primary Teacher, Chris was Head of Geography at a large Comprehensive School. We were enjoying our lifestyle with a newborn son, three acres of daffodils and a greenhouse. Progression in Teaching usually leads to less time in the classroom and greater administration. This did not appeal to Chris. Jan's key decision was whether or not to resign her full-time post and raise a family or return to work after Maternity Leave. We evolved a joint solution; a job-share of Jan's post. If the proposal had been accepted, we would have shared Jan's Primary School class, each of us teaching to our strengths and being able to fully commit to education; the school children would benefit with the infusion of new drive and energy from each of us.

In the 1980s, job-share was a relatively new concept and Headteachers and Governors responsible for appointments would have probably perceived the idea as revolutionary. We regarded this as an opportunity missed. Looking back, we could have mounted a 'campaign', enlisting support. Instead, we put our energy into other career developments over the succeeding years. This eventually materialised into purchasing over 500 square metres of derelict Cornish barn complex in 1996 which we would convert into a large Children's Nursery and a home.

Amalgamation of Children's Nursery with Primary Schools

Rather like the 'Marks and Spencer' Christmas food advert, our Nursery wasn't just a Children's Nursery, it was a special Nursery. We thought very carefully about what captures children's imaginations and as Teachers we were well aware of the educational requirements in Early Years development. Our role as providers was to make this as exciting and inclusive as possible, creating an enduring impact; with a suite of barns, a large animal house, several fields, a stream and even a vineyard, we considered that we had the edge over what was currently provided in other Pre-school settings including primary schools and playgroups.

When we started the Nursery in 1997, four-year olds were provided with places at nurseries, schools and playgroups via Government grants. This was eventually provided to three-year olds. Most parents valued the 'free' places and private nurseries and playgroups thrived in East Cornwall. Today, there are few if any and virtually all pre-school children are now in Early Years settings in primary schools. We provided such a unique experience but could not hold back this political tide.

Our second light bulb moment: What if we were to be integrated into an educational bubble, owned or funded by the Local Educational Authority as an outreach centre for pupils in East Cornwall? This idea was not successful; the light bulb dimmed.

In 2004 we started the search for a building plot, which we eventually found in 2014. In the meantime, a set of Grade II Listed barns in North Cornwall caught our eye.

Building on an Old Farmhouse Site

It has been mentioned in the Introduction to this book that our second major build, a pair of Grade II Listed barns, had construction issues. Our Structural Engineering report returned a very negative conclusion concerning the ability to achieve the proposed first floor indicated in the Planning Permission. We promptly withdrew our offer on the property, but it didn't prevent us from thinking 'outside the box'. Investigating 19th century maps, it was obvious that most of the associated farm: the main farmhouse, the linhay barn and the cruciform mill barn were all constructed at this time. These buildings were part of the expansion of Cornwall's farms on a commercial scale. The linhay itself was built in the 1860s and provided ample parking space underneath for trailers and equipment, with perhaps hay/timber stored on the first floor.

The light bulb moment came when we realised that within the boundaries of the linhay plot were the foundations of the original pre-19th century farmhouse. These foundations still had some of the cob* walls on them. A well and the original track to the farmhouse was also located nearby. Additionally, next to the farmhouse footprint was 'Orchard Barn' which is altogether on a much smaller scale, with room for half a dozen cattle on the ground floor and two pairs of double doors on the first floor for manual threshing. If the linhay was structurally difficult, why not

_____

* Cob: a mixture of soil, straw/horse-hair and sometimes lime mixed with water, traditionally used to build walls.

build on the site of the original farmhouse? This would be out of sight from the end of the parish road and we could use the linhay barn as it was originally intended, vehicular storage without worrying about the first floor problems. We were very positive with the Planners in a pre-planning conversation; but they insisted that this would create new development in the countryside. The fact that they had already given permanent Planning Permission for the linhay had escaped them. We suggested that we wanted in effect to transfer the residential Planning Permission over to the former old farmhouse site which would have maintained the historical significance of the linhay. Once again the light bulb dimmed.

The linhay was a wonderful barn that seduced us. We went back to the drawing board, had involved conversations with the Conservation Officer and evolved a complex solution with our builder who was confident about overcoming the problems.

All three light bulb ideas were borne out of perceived necessity; all three pushed the boundaries of accepted practice of the time and all three got the 'thumbs down' from the various authorities. On each occasion we moved on, not allowing setbacks to restrict our aspirations. Conversely, if we had taken each challenge further, the job-share, the Nursery amalgamation and the old farmhouse plot, who knows where we would be now?

CONCLUSION

We make many major decisions in life, including career choice, partners, marriage, children, emigration etc. Surely, to self-build would be within the top ten and 'should not be entered into lightly'. Our purpose in writing this book was to present a balanced view to enable you to make an informed decision if you aspire to building your own home. Those who have already completed a self-build will no doubt identify with our experiences; you may merely enjoy stories of human courage with meaningful photographs. This book is not a technical manual; such detail can be gleaned from the references and the internet. We have tried to point out the sacrifices that are necessary and what you can realistically expect along the route, with a degree of honesty that is often lacking elsewhere. The 'telly-builders' are very brave people because they add to all the pressures of a build by telling the World. Some of the personal and professional partnerships do not survive and it is tragic if a build is ultimately responsible for a personal break up.

Self-building your own home is rewarding. Let's face it, if investing large sums of money, great chunks of time and taking on the inevitable stresses and strains, then a substantial return is expected. If all goes well, the building that you may well have designed and built will give you an immense sense of achievement, particularly when reinforced by positive comments from others. Aside from job satisfaction, your house will probably be larger and of a higher specification than you would otherwise have afforded by merely purchasing one. Financially, the house should be worth more than the sum of all the components and labour. We could add that self-building can also be fun, although this is far from being a universal experience.

Like a good novel, your self-build journey will start with a plot. Our ten-year plot search was probably exceptional and towards the end of this, the concept of a green patch of land was changing to other possibilities. We considered buildings that could be extended or even knocked down and multi plots that could be subdivided. This book demonstrates that, even when residential Planning Permission exists on a plot, there can be significant issues to overcome.

During the Covid epidemic, people were encouraged to work from home where possible. Large numbers of the population could choose how, where and when to work with the bonus of a great reduction in commuting. This appears to have translated into a growing enthusiasm for moving to the countryside. The West Country has seen a growing demand for housing which has boosted house prices. This is in contrast to the pessimistic predictions of Brexit. Whatever the outcome of these pressures on house prices, the self-builder should not rely on optimistic forecasts. We do hope that the 2016 'Right to Build' legislation* for England, will help to moderate plot prices by increasing the availability.

If you are contemplating self-build, then take a look in the mirror and meet the Boss! Conventional employments have managers that often set targets for the benefit of the organisation. You are the Boss, the driving force and your project will succeed or fail due to your leadership. Setting targets along a time line is essential. Missing a target will interrupt the sequence and the reset button will have to be pressed with the inevitable time and financial penalties. Spreadsheets offer logical sequencing reassurance, but be realistic about the timing of each stage.

Self-build is all about your heart and mind. Yes, we are talking mainly budget here! Build the house that you can realistically

---

* Housing and Planning Act requires Local Authorities to maintain a register of people wishing to build/create their own home. See: www. righttobuildportal.org.uk

afford, remembering to include a generous contingency. Do not let your heart wholly determine your build; equally, your budget should not be the ogre that creates negativity. Try to keep to your budget throughout the build, bearing in mind that overspends early on will lead to compromises later, which may impact on finishes that determine the overall appearance of your house.

Once you have completed the build, moved in and are enjoying the spaces, many of the memories of hardship will fade; your home will heal the wounds. Photographs will tell the tale of the good and the not-so-good days. It gives us pleasure to display iconic images of our builds on our walls. Many people will eventually move from their 'forever home'(!) and it is a thoughtful idea to provide the new owners with a photographic technical record as well as a history of the building.

In this oak frame build, we feel that we have done our little bit to slow down global warming by reducing our carbon footprint. Government incentives genuinely encouraged us to 'go green' on the choice of an Air Source Heat Pump. We would however like the Government to go a great deal further in encouraging the self-builder (see Appendix 1, Open Letter to Government). The Green Revolution heralded to kick-start the post-Covid period, should help here. Had the one million Brits who aspired to build their own home within the year 2019-20 (build-review.com, April '19) proceeded, what a reduction that would have made to our National housing shortage.

We have genuinely enjoyed building three major projects amounting to in excess of 1,000 square metres in Cornwall over a twenty-five year period. Our two previous barn conversions involved exemplary examples of 19th century Cornish farm buildings. In the Introduction, we stated that you need to possess 'a degree of tenacity' if you wish to self-build. This inner determination is evident on three levels: there are the scary moments, the challenging periods and the days to be endured. Countersuing our first Architect on our initial barn conversion can only be described as scary and the Appeal against the Planning

Refusal in the oak frame house came a close second, especially when the implications of failure were contemplated. Our 'challenging' category includes items such as getting the best price on materials, informing tradespeople not to annoy the neighbours, as per the digger driver, not to mention the slate circle! Finally, you have to lead by motivational example on a daily basis. You will be tested on those cold, wet, grey days!

In writing this book, we have become reflective. In our previous careers as Teachers, we always encouraged children to have a go. We hope that we have left a positive legacy of motivated people. Now, through our buildings, we offer a more tangible product, still with an inspirational zeal. Ask yourself where you want to be in five years' time and if the answer is a resounding: "Living in my self-build house!", then plan accordingly and don't rush into it until you are totally convinced. Listen to others, especially the positive ones; but above all, give it your total energy because it will need that and then some. GOOD LUCK!

Our key aim: harmonious with the surrounding landscape?

APPENDIX 1

Self-build and Government

Building your own home will involve countless official contacts which we have deemed 'Government'. When everything runs smoothly, all is well; the rants start when you perceive that officialdom have somehow got it wrong. We would like to make some humble suggestions that would make the self-builder's life both easier and fairer.

There is one other point to mention. Self-builders do not have a strong voice to Government because we are an ever-changing, short-term group. Our builds will be long completed by the time that any constructive suggestions to the systems would materialise; so why get involved?

We suggest an open letter to the Government, probably via your local MP. We have included some of the most irritating aspects of officialdom. It has been our experience in both our Teaching and Building careers that any changes in the system invariably benefit the 'organisation' not the individual.

1. Our Planning Permission Refusal

We were refused Planning Permission on the oak frame by the Local Authority. We Appealed the decision and won the case; but it cost us in time and money. There was no financial compensation. This system should be reviewed urgently.

2. Local Authority Building Control (LABC)

The current system for Inspections is that the LABC will send an available Officer. We would much prefer an assigned Officer for the duration of the build. LABC Officers are a font of knowledge and they would get to know the building and the builders.

3. Walk-in Planning Advice

In the good old days you could walk in to a local Planning Office and have a chat with the 'Duty Planner'. This has now morphed into the 'Pre-app', a semi-formal Application involving more cost and time and is ultimately not binding.

4. VAT

We would like to sit down with Government Officials, each of us writing out a list of all the costs involved in building a new house. We cannot understand why the VAT charged for Professional Services such as Architects, Tree Surveyors, Building Control and Structural Engineers, cannot be refunded. Furthermore, try building a house without sandpaper, white spirit and disinfectant. We want the VAT back on reasonable consumables.

The Treasury collects VAT on a quarterly basis from businesses. Why can't self-builders similarly claim VAT refunds every three months? Currently you wait until the end of the build for a one-off claim. This could be many years. Is this fair?

5. Council Tax Assessment

There appears to be huge confusion over this between various Authorities. Can it be correct that the Local Authority is able to claim Council Tax on buildings that cannot be legally rented due to the absence of key facilities such as a kitchen or bathroom? It would be helpful to have a more uniform system nationally, defining levels of acceptable habitation, enabling self-builders to move into partially completed properties with an appropriate intermediate Assessment of Council Tax Band.

Self-builders are adding to the Nation's housing stock. We hope that the above issues are urgently reviewed both to smooth the route through the minefield of paperwork and to make the current system fairer for some very hardworking, determined self-builders.

APPENDIX 2

List of Suppliers (In Approximate Build Order)

The Green Oak Carpentry Company Ltd, GU33 7JW

Richard Ward, Pentargon Architecture, PL15 8SA

Evolve Tree Consultancy, TR1 2QE

Acland Plant Hire, TR4 8HP

Colin Marshall Scaffolding, PL25 3TA

Fahey's Concrete, PL24 2SX

Parkway Timber Co. Ltd, PL30 4BB

J J Smith & Co. Joinery Ltd, TR3 6PQ

Rangemoors, EX19 8DW

Tinhay, PL15 8EX

Adept Glaziers Ltd, TR3 7JQ

Graham Barker Roofing Services Ltd, PL26 8LX

Howdens, TR1 2XR

Tile Wise Ltd, TR1 2DP

Gateway Tile & Slate Ltd, PL15 8EX

Contec South West Ltd, PL25 5RJ

Morgan Masonry Ltd, TR3 6LG

Harvest Cornwall Ltd, TR7 2QT

Camel Glass & Joinery Ltd, PL27 6HB

Cornwall Hardwood Supplies, Camborne

Screwfix, TR1 2ST

Western Electrical, TR1 3LP

Mick Stone Building Supplies, PL27 6AG

City Plumbing Supplies, TR1 2XN

Lawer Bros. Ltd, TR10 9AF

Continental Underfloor, PL15 7PJ

Home Supply Retail Ltd, PL4 0ST

Builders Merchants: D R Building Materials, Jewson, RGB, Travis Perkins

.

APPENDIX 3

Further Reading

Building Your Own Home
David Snell and Murray Armor
Random House UK, 18ᵗʰ edition 2006
ISBN: 978-0-09188-619-6

Green Oak in Construction
Peter Ross, Christopher Mettem and Andrew Holloway
TRADA Technology Ltd. 2007
ISBN: 978-1900510-45-5

Oak-Framed Buildings
Rupert Newman
The Guild of Master Craftsman Publications Ltd. 2014
ISBN: 978-1-86108-726-3

The Site Manager's Bible
Len Sales
Ebury Press 2007
ISBN: 9780091909079

Homebuilding & Renovating (Monthly Magazine)
Future Publishing Ltd
ISBN: 9 770960 086215

A Year in Provence
Peter Mayle
Penguin Random House UK 2000
ISBN: 978-0-14-029603-7

Special Mention

Guedelon: A Castle in the Making
Maryline Martin and Florian Renucci
Ouest-France
ISBN: 978-2-7373-6996-4
(A well-presented example of experimental castle-building in France which we found inspiring whilst building on a more humble scale.)

LITERARY WORKS IN PROGRESS

■ ■ ■ ▪ ▪

Our series of three books have been inspired by the reminiscing and reflecting on our 25 years of self-building. These two further texts represent a melting pot of ideas and memories. They are starting points for detailing the many aspects of searching, preparing, building, living and finally selling the two barn complexes that preceded the current new-build.

'The Linhay' Conversion Project

The building works completed in 2011 on this Grade II Listed, 19th century barn are featured in the second book of our trilogy: 'We Built .... in Cornwall'. The project which we took on in the absence of a building plot, actually consisted of two barns, adding to the complexity.

We can still remember the characteristic chuckle of incredulity from some estate agents in Cornwall when enquiring about available building plots! Compromise; we had barn conversion experience .... how about this as an alternative to a green site? It was actually 'love at first site (sight)'! .... The linhay barn was a truly wonderful building that had 'seduced' us. Strangely, it didn't appear to be typically Cornish. This became an intriguing story ending with the cream and jam debate on scones!

What do you do when a Structural Engineer tells you to leave well alone, walk away or else regret it? Something about us .... this was a challenge. Was it as romantic as a crusade to save a building?

Grade II buildings attract Conservation Officers; they also cherish old buildings. However, they have strict rules. We were not permitted to raise the roof to achieve the two storeys given in the approved Planning Permission; but going down was acceptable. One of our milestones was not 'getting out of the ground', rather getting into it.

Small spaces require small machines; even smaller spaces require shovels!

Do not underestimate your role as Project Manager/Owner; it can sometimes involve being something of a father figure.

A dank, dark former Blacksmith's shop was converted to perhaps our most successful space. We now know what a flitch beam is.

The much older and smaller, ancillary barn which we named 'Orchard Barn' would provide 'quick fix ' accommodation while converting the main barn; but there was an older footprint of a building to be investigated which could change everything.

One large barn plus one small barn lends itself to multi-generational living. The issue: Who gets what and is that always fair?

Barn Complex Conversion Project: Children's Nursery and House

We go back further in time to the late 1990s, the first of our builds: 500 square metres of iconic, 19th century Cornish barns. We were keen, enthusiastic and rather 'green' in our lack of experience and there were but a few voices of approval to our excited vision amongst our friends and family. Was this a mid-life educational crisis?

Unusually, the complex was not Listed; but the Duchy of Cornwall had similar restrictions, even dictating the colour of the external joinery! There were two main barns, configured in an 'L' shape. The first to be converted into a Children's Nursery, was to be the income provider. Jan planned the Nursery while Chris continued with his full-time Teaching. It was necessary to employ a Project Manager for this Nursery phase. We experienced difficulties with the Architect in this first major part of the build. What lessons did we learn from the process?

Our first caravan living experience on site.

A valuable lesson was learned in double-checking that crucial instructions had been forwarded to the concrete supplier; you order a lorry full of concrete for a specified time and three turn up at once!

A provision for children or plants? One caller was clearly confused!

Who turned the lights out? (Total Solar Eclipse 1999)

That noise really was a bomb being detonated!

Dendrochronology research at Sheffield University; big word, small tree rings to accurately date the wood used in a building.

Our donkey connection with the Royal Cornwall Show; it all started with a donkey certification course for the whole family.

Messy, wet, steamy and unbelievably exciting; that was the scene of our first lamb being born, watched over by a local farmer with an audience of young children, parents, Teachers and Nursery Nurses. Nothing 'virtual' here!

The large collection of animals which also included rabbits and goats, the stream channel, complete with locks and boat harbour play area, the vegetable garden, vineyard and the open spaces of the fields were a haven of sensory experiences for children.

Our barns were originally part of a former country estate and we reconnected with it through our sheep, our dog and even through a unique musical experience that was perpetuated for almost a decade.

These reflections over three builds are not works of fiction and we were not always in control of events. Our biggest project was tackled with the smallest amount of experience. 'Self-build' is never literally that. Typically, there are so many others involved. It is a large financial process, often taking years. Yes, there are rewards, none more so than standing back and declaring: "We built that!" We felt that we had saved some truly amazing pieces of agricultural architecture, by creating a viable function. Don't self-build because others did and succeeded. Self-build because of the dream, the passion, almost the primaeval desire to put a roof over your head, but also have total regard for that wise Irish saying:

> 'May the roof above you never fall in,
> And those gathered beneath it never fall out.'

We wish you every success.

If you have found this first book of the trilogy, inspirational, instructive and entertaining, we would be thrilled if you could write an encouraging review on one of the usual sites such as Amazon, Waterstones or other purchasing source. It is our mission to steer many an enthusiast through the intricate route that is self-build.

Thank you.
Chris and Jan Stevens
June 2021

Lightning Source UK Ltd.
Milton Keynes UK
UKHW020413130721
387042UK00001B/10